The Case for Universal
Basic Services

Anna Coote
Andrew Percy

———————

The Case for Universal Basic Services

polity

First published in 2020 by Polity Press

Polity Press
65 Bridge Street
Cambridge CB2 1UR, UK

Polity Press
101 Station Landing
Suite 300
Medford, MA 02155, USA

ISBN-13: 978-1-5095-3982-6
ISBN-13: 978-1-5095-3983-3 (pb)

A catalogue record for this book is available from the British Library.

Library of Congress Cataloging-in-Publication Data

Names: Coote, Anna, author. | Percy, Andrew, author.
Title: The case for universal basic services / Anna Coote, Andrew Percy.
Description: Cambridge, UK ; Medford, MA : Polity, 2020. | Series: The case for | Summary: "The idea that healthcare and education should be provided as universal public services to all who need them is widely accepted. But why leave it there? Why not expand it to more of life's essentials? In this bold new book, Anna Coote and Andrew Percy argue that Universal Basic Services is exactly what we need to save our societies and our planet"-- Provided by publisher.
Identifiers: LCCN 2019028827 (print) | LCCN 2019028828 (ebook) | ISBN 9781509539826 (hardback) | ISBN 9781509539833 (paperback) | ISBN 9781509539840 (epub)
Subjects: LCSH: Social policy. | Basic needs--Government policy.
Classification: LCC HV91 .C6759 2020   (print) | LCC HV91   (ebook) | DDC 320.6--dc23
LC record available at https://lccn.loc.gov/2019028827
LC ebook record available at https://lccn.loc.gov/2019028828

Typeset in 11 on 15 Sabon by Servis Filmsetting Ltd, Stockport, Cheshire
Printed and bound in the UK by TJ International Limited

For further information on Polity, visit our website: politybooks.com

Contents

Acknowledgements

We are extremely grateful to Ian Gough for invaluable advice and support throughout, to Pritika Kasliwal and Edanur Yazici for their research, and to Alfie Stirling for helpful feedback on the draft. We are also indebted to Henrietta Moore and the Institute for Global Prosperity for their work on developing the idea of UBS.

Introduction

All of us, however much or little we earn, need certain things to make our lives possible – and worth living. A roof over our heads, nourishing food, education, people to look after us when we can't look after ourselves, health care when we are ill, water and electricity, transport to take us where we need to go and (these days) access to the internet.

We also need money so that we can pay for some of these things directly, such as food, rent and utility bills, although sometimes we cannot afford them. We pay for other things, such as education and roads, indirectly through taxes because we could never afford to buy them outright unless we were very rich. In the United Kingdom, the National Health Service provides free health care at the point of need, so you do not have to worry about the cost of treatment or buying private health insurance. In most rich countries, there are some things that you don't need to pay for directly because they are collectively provided – although free services sometimes fall short of adequate.

What all these things have in common is that they are everyday essentials that everybody needs to live a decent life.

Suppose, then, that we all clubbed together and made sure they were available and affordable for everyone. Suppose we pooled our resources so that the risk of suffering the ruinous consequences of going without one or more of these essentials was shared between us. That's the goal of universal basic services (UBS): acting together to help each other, and ourselves, so that everyone has access to three things that are fundamental to a successful, peaceful, functioning democracy: security, opportunity and participation.

It is not exactly a new idea. It echoes the ambitions of Roosevelt's New Deal in the 1930s and the UK post-war settlement. Both were based on the premise that the whole of society is responsible for – and dependent upon – the well-being of every member of society. Therefore, governments were compelled to act against the scourge of unemployment and poverty and to combat the associated evils of illness, squalid housing and poor education. Funds were gathered through taxes and national insurance schemes to pay for schools, health care, housing and income support for those unable to earn – and all this helped to generate employment and a productive economy. As well as take-home pay, people received a virtual income in the form of public services. This has been described as part of a 'social wage' that includes state pensions and benefits. It was worth a great deal to everyone, and especially to those on low incomes, because it met their needs and did not have to be paid for directly.

We still have a virtual income or 'social wage' today, but it is much diminished and misunder stood. After the economic disruptions of the 1970s, government policies have chipped away at the post-war consensus and at the value of the social wage. They have done this by promoting a vision of economic success based on personal choice, private ownership, a small state and a free market, blaming the jobless and poor for their own troubles and urging individuals to help themselves. Since 2008, the effects in many countries have been ratcheted up by tax cuts and severely reduced public spending. Where the quality of free schools and health care has declined as a result, more people are encouraged to leave the public system and pay privately for what they need. Many services, including care for children and disabled adults, as well as housing and transport, have been stripped down to the bare bones, abolished altogether or left to the vagaries of voluntarism and philanthropy. This steady erosion of services, often combined with cuts to the value of social security benefits, has led to a deepening rift between rich and poor and to millions living in destitution in the world's richest countries.

It doesn't have to be like this. Our goal is to reclaim the collective ideal and rebuild the social wage. Let's start by defining our terms.

'Universal basic services' (UBS) encapsulates three crucial concepts. What we mean by each of them is best described in reverse order. Together they sum up what we mean by 'public services' whenever we refer to them in the following pages:

1 *Services*: collectively generated activities that serve the public interest.[1]
2 *Basic*: services that are essential and sufficient (rather than minimal) to enable people to meet their needs.
3 *Universal*: everyone is entitled to services that are sufficient to meet their needs, regardless of ability to pay.

Introduction

Central to our case is that UBS should be expanded in practice, both by improving the quality of existing services such as health care and education, and reaching into new areas such as care, housing, transport and access to digital information.

We are seeking radical change that builds on the best we already have. We don't want to return to the 'good old days' or simply to have more of what we've had in the past. Our proposal is radical for three main reasons. First, central to our case is the *collective ideal*, which has been submerged and discredited by the politics of individual choice and market competition. We aim to reverse that trend, recognizing that what we do together and how we care for each other is the key to enabling all of us to meet our needs and live lives that we value.

Second, we aim for *sufficiency and sustainability*. Universal basic services form an essential part of an agenda for sustainable development, which we must embrace as a matter of priority to safeguard the future of human civilization.

Third, we are seeking to *overhaul the traditional model of public services* so that they are genuinely participative, controlled by the people who need and use them, and supported rather than always directly provided by the state.

We need these radical changes now, not just

because we want to help make people's lives better (which we do) but because we are convinced that this is the only way for modern societies to survive and flourish. Existing welfare systems are struggling to meet today's needs. They haven't adapted far or fast enough to demographic, technological and ecological challenges. They have come under sustained attack from political forces that seek to shrink the state and grow the market. People are being driven apart by an ideology that promotes individualism, competition and accumulation, which in turn have stifled aspirations, heightened insecurities, exacerbated environmental problems and accelerated political polarization. All these things undermine democracies, which depend for their health and strength on shared interests and goals, mutual understanding and cooperation.

We want this book to fuel a big debate about how to tackle today's urgent problems, such as widening inequalities, crumbling welfare systems and unsustainable consumption. We focus here on a particular range of needs to illustrate our approach. But we certainly do not want to limit the scope of UBS, which could extend much further. As we shall see, it is not about applying a single plan of action to all of life's necessities but about adopting a set of value-based guidelines and customizing them to suit a variety of different needs and circumstances.

The term UBS was first given voice in October 2017 in a report from the Institute for Global Prosperity, University College London.[2] It offers an approach that is distinct from 'universal basic income' (UBI). The latter is a proposal to give regular, unconditional cash payments to everyone, rich and poor – ostensibly to reduce poverty and inequality, promote opportunities and solve problems arising from ungenerous, stigmatizing systems of income support. We wholeheartedly endorse the principle that everyone should have the right to a minimum income and that no one should suffer blame or stigma for falling on hard times. Radical reform of income support, although not the topic of this book, is extremely urgent. But the solution to the problem of inadequate social security is not 'UBI', universal, unconditional cash payments that are sufficient to live on, which is how it is defined by many of its leading advocates. We can find no evidence that UBI could ever live up to the more ambitious claims that are made for it.[3]

On the other hand, we are convinced that UBS holds out real promise for achieving similar goals. Instead of plugging into the neoliberal formula of individual consumption within a market-based system, UBS offers a collective approach that supplements – and reduces dependence on – individual monetary income. As we argue later, more and better public services can deliver far better results in terms of equality, efficiency, solidarity and sustainability.

1

Why We Need This Change

No one should have to pay for emergency health care or endure a three-week wait to see a local doctor. Every parent should feel confident that their children will be happy and well educated at the local (non-fee-paying) school. There should be no need for food banks or rough sleeping, no graphs showing widening health inequalities or rising levels of mental distress.

These are not outrageous imaginings, just reasonable expectations of anyone living in a modern democracy. Yet too many live with basic insecurities, too few parents are confident about local schooling, and too many doubt they will get decent health care when they need it. And while these worries are shared by people on average incomes, it is much worse for those who are poorer.

Homelessness, extreme poverty and despair are all on the rise.

When the United Nations sent a Special Rapporteur on Extreme Poverty and Human Rights to the United States in 2017, he found that none of its manifestly superior wealth, power and technology was being 'harnessed to address the situation in which 40 million people continue to live in poverty'. He concluded that the persistence of extreme poverty was 'a political choice made by those in power'.[1] When the same Rapporteur visited the United Kingdom in 2018, he found, similarly, that it was 'patently unjust and contrary to British values' that so many people were living in poverty in the world's fifth-largest economy; it was not an inevitable consequence of economic forces, he said, but the choice of a government committed to 'radical social re-engineering'.[2] The United States and the United Kingdom may have moved further in this direction than other rich countries, but there have been comparable shifts in government priorities, public attitudes and spending patterns across the rich world.

The case for UBS is about choosing another direction. It rests on two key principles: *shared needs* and *collective responsibilities*. These don't belong to the neoliberal 'common sense' that has shaped our politics for too many decades. But they strike such a deep chord in our everyday experience and familiar feelings that, when you get to thinking about them, they are altogether more common and more sensible. They are also soundly anchored in political theory.

All human beings have the same set of basic needs that must be satisfied in order to survive and thrive, think for ourselves and participate in society. Theories of capability and human need converge around this point. Martha Nussbaum describes three 'core' capabilities: of affiliation, bodily integrity and practical reason.[3] Len Doyal and Ian Gough identify health and critical autonomy as basic human needs that are prerequisites for social participation.[4]

These basic human needs are universal across time and space. Of course, the practical detail of how they are satisfied will vary widely, as norms, resources and expectations shift and change between generations and countries. But there are certain generic categories of universal 'intermediate needs' that are more enduring. These are the means by which we meet our basic needs. They have been listed by need theorists as water, nutrition, shelter, secure and non-threatening work, education, health care, security in childhood, significant primary relationships, physical and economic security, and a safe environment.[5] Unlike basic needs, intermediate needs may evolve over time. For example, recent efforts to identify 'a set of universal, irreducible and essential set of material conditions for achieving basic human wellbeing' have found that access to motorized transport and to information and communications could be added the list.[6]

Needs are not like wants. Wants vary infinitely and can multiply exponentially. If you don't get what you want, you won't die or cease to be part of human society, but that could happen if you don't get what you need. Needs cannot usually be substituted for one another (a lack of water and shelter cannot be offset by more education or health care). They are part of an essential package. And needs are satiable: there are limits beyond which more food, more work or more security are no longer helpful and could even do you harm. There comes a point where *sufficiency* is reached in the process of meeting needs. By contrast, there will never come a time when we all have everything we want.

Understanding the difference between needs and wants or preferences provides an enduring, evidence-based and ethical foundation for making decisions about what things are truly essential for the survival and well-being of everyone, now and in future. It doesn't trap us in any kind of uniform determinism because we acknowledge that history, geography, politics and culture shape the specific ways in which needs are satisfied. But it helps us to set priorities that are more, rather than less, likely to be fair and sustainable.

As individuals today, we can meet some of our needs through market transactions, depending on our circumstances. Food and clothing are examples here: most of us expect to be able to buy these ourselves, and having enough money to do this is clearly important. There are other needs that most of us cannot meet without help and we depend on others for our capacity to do so. Health care and education are the most common examples but, as we shall argue, the range of needs requiring a collective response is much wider. If we are to live together in society, we are all responsible for ensuring that everyone's basic needs are met – through a combination of measures to support income and provide services. As the sociologist Emile Durkheim observed, people 'cannot live together without agreeing and consequently without making mutual sacrifices, joining themselves to one another in a strong and enduring fashion'. This is not just a worthy option, but the 'fundamental basis' of social life.[7]

Roosevelt's New Deal and post-war welfare states involved pooling resources and sharing risks through the institutions of government. Most post-war settlements aimed to achieve full (male) employment, to provide income support for those who could not earn and to supply necessities that people could not afford to pay for individually in the form of public services that were free at the point of use. The political philosopher T. H. Marshall summed up the collective approach in the concept of 'social citizenship', which held that every member of society had *positive* economic and social rights as well as the more traditional *'negative'* rights that protected us from harm and maintained our civil liberties.[8]

Social citizenship is anchored in both ethical and practical considerations. People are to be helped by their fellow citizens, rather than blamed and punished if they fall on hard times; and a thriving population is good for the economy. Civil and political rights cannot be realized unless people have sufficient social and economic means to live and act. Collective responsibility implies mutual obligations as well as rights. It's a dynamic process where everyone gives and receives. Yet people cannot fulfil their obligations unless their basic needs are met.

This interdependence provides the moral foundation for every human society. The 'moral economy' underpins the material economy and 'embodies norms and sentiments regarding the responsibilities and rights of individuals and institutions with regard to others'.[9]

The collective provision of services to meet shared needs is worth as much or more to us than the money we earn through employment. Most simply, it is a virtual income that replaces out-of-pocket expenditure, leaving us more disposable cash. This is the virtual income or 'social wage' we referred to earlier. It's a notion that can be traced back many decades, but it is too rarely discussed today. The economic historian R. H. Tawney observed that 'the standard of living of the great mass of the nation depends, not merely on the remuneration which they are paid for their labour, but on the social income which they receive as citizens'.[10]

The full worth of the social wage is even greater than its monetary replacement cost. It yields value indirectly and over time through the effects of services on others, not just ourselves, and on society as a whole. Furthermore, there is an important dimension of its value that does not feature in the theories of Durkheim, Marshall or Tawney but is inescapable today.

This is the imperative for human activity to

remain within the ecological constraints of a finite planet. Unless we heed the scientists' predictions, there is real danger that, within a matter of decades, there will be no recognizable human society for which to plan or deliver public services. Therefore any policy proposal that aims to improve human well-being must be designed to reduce harmful emissions, safeguard natural resources and stay within safe planetary boundaries.

As we shall argue, the fact that UBS is rooted in shared needs and collective responsibilities makes it far better placed to achieve sustainable practice than any welfare system based on market values and individual payments. It provides value not just for today but into the future, for generations to come. This accords with the most frequently quoted definition of sustainable development, in the 1987 Brundtland Report, as meeting 'the needs of the present without compromising the ability of future generations to meet their own needs'.[11]

2

How Would It Work in Practice?

What could UBS look like in practice? Think of the UK National Health Service (NHS). It is more than 70 years old and still going strong. It offers health care to all who need it, free at the point of use and paid for through taxation. It's far from perfect. It has been plagued by successive governments' attempts to reorganize its management structures and to introduce for-profit contractors and private finance. This has all been done in the name of improving efficiency and getting better outcomes for patients, but in fact waiting times have lengthened, there are growing staff shortages and there is a widening 'health gap' between different areas and social groups, with poor people getting ill more often and dying younger than rich people. Still, the NHS is hanging in there, a national treasure, commanding huge public support. A survey in 2017 by the King's Fund found that 77% of the public believe that the NHS should be maintained in its current form and around 90% support its founding principles: that the NHS should meet the needs of everyone, be free at the point of delivery and based on clinical need, not the ability to pay.[1]

Free schooling is another pillar of the post-war settlement, badly shaken in some places, but still standing. Education can make a huge difference to health and well-being. Potentially, schools are an extremely powerful way of meeting many of our shared needs. In the United Kingdom and many other countries, public spending per pupil has been cut, teachers are stretched beyond limits and the chances of poor children getting exam results that compare well with their richer peers are low and declining. Yet a recent survey of social attitudes found that four-fifths (80%) of respondents reported having at least some confidence in the British school system.[2]

The goal of more and better public services certainly calls for more public funds (we'll come to that in chapter 6), but it doesn't mean just pumping more money into failed systems, however treasured they may be. What these two examples show is, first, that we already have a rich experience of UBS in practice, and there is plenty to learn from both the failings and the successes of that experience. Second, services differ from each other because of the specific functions they perform to meet needs. Each one requires a customized approach.

We expect UBS to include radical improvements in health care, schooling and other existing services, such as policing, which are already free and universal in many countries. Beyond that, we want to reach into areas where life's essentials are not yet provided, so that everyone has an equal chance to fulfil their potential and participate in society.

We start by distinguishing between what the Manchester School's work on the foundational economy describes as the material and the providential economy.[3] The material realm is mainly about *things*, such as roads, railways, pipes and cables, public buildings and vehicles. The providential realm primarily involves *human interaction*, such as in health care, education and other caring and relational services and activities. Both kinds of infrastructure comprise everyday necessities that are often invisible or taken for granted; they rarely get noticed until something goes wrong with them. The two are interdependent and can be hard to disentangle – for example, education and caring services need facilities and equipment, while railway lines are useless without train services, and gas pipes need to be maintained.

To give focus to our proposal, we have decided to home in on the providential and on the areas where there has been most public debate about the harm caused by the absence or inadequacy of universal services. These are (in no order of priority) child care, adult social care, housing, transport and access to digital information. We must stress that the scope of the UBS agenda could be much wider: these are just examples.

UBS is not a silver bullet or a one-size-fits-all solution to the challenge of exercising collective responsibility. It is a complex proposition with multiple dimensions. So we start by exploring the complexities to understand how each area requires a customized approach and what features they have in common.

Responsibility

First, there is the question of where responsibility lies. Responsibility, in this context, means having a duty or obligation to carry out a function and be held accountable for it. The post-war settlement recognized collective responsibility and located it with the state so that services were provided directly by national or local government. Many services, notably adult social care, are now commissioned by governments from private or third-sector organizations, with varying arrangements for regulation. Charities and NGOs have sometimes stepped in to provide services abandoned by government: local youth services are an example. Some amenities, such as sports clubs and swimming pools, have been largely privatized. As a result, responsibilities are increasingly attenuated, spread out in various combinations, with government, commercial businesses, non-profit, charitable and voluntary organizations assuming different degrees of responsibility in different settings.

At the same time, there have been calls for individuals, families and local groups to take more responsibility and depend less on the state for meeting their needs. These come from different parts of the political spectrum, as we shall see. Those who use or may need services have been cast variously as users, clients, customers, consumers, partners or participants, signalling different relationships and degrees of responsibility.[4]

Power and devolution

Questions about responsibility are closely linked with questions about power. The traditional top-down model of public provision has been criticized for disempowering people who use services, discouraging civic and familial mutual aid, and encouraging dependence. Advocates of market values, as well as some groups of services users, have claimed that people are empowered by exercising choice. However, experience has shown that, unless everyone has similar amounts of information, skills and confidence, choice will empower the better off and better educated. And choice is often illusory because there is little or nothing to choose between.

Meanwhile, some commercial organizations have accumulated power by growing their share of contracted-out services. Regulation is often too light or ineffective, allowing a few heavyweights to dominate the market.

There is substantial support for devolving power to local areas and for applying the principle of 'subsidiarity' (exercising power at the lowest level possible to achieve defined goals). This ambition – as with calls for shifting responsibility towards individuals and communities – is shared by widely differing political tendencies, with various interpretations. For those on the right, the aim is to shift responsibility and power away from central government to locally based businesses, charities and other non-government organizations, and to reduce centralized funding or withdraw it altogether.[5] Around the political centre, 'localism' means shifting power from the national or federal level to local government bodies and boosting their capacity to raise funds, so that they can ensure that their constituents' needs are met – either directly or in partnership with other local organizations and residents.[6]

Communitarians and some supporters of the 'commoning' movement want to encourage independent, local groups to take control of services, which they define and manage for themselves. Within these groups, there is a strong anti-state strand of politics, which sees government as part of the problem, not the solution, and favours local self-determination and self-organization as the preferred alternative to both state and market.[7] Others favour devolution of power to local areas and want much more control in the hands of residents than some protagonists of localism, but they seek to achieve this within a democratic framework where the state retains key responsibilities (set out below) – this is roughly where we stand.

How Would It Work in Practice?

Ownership

Beyond direct state ownership, there is a wide range of models for organizations providing services. These include multinational corporations, small and medium-sized businesses, social enterprises, cooperatives and mutuals, user-led organizations, registered charities and community groups organized around neighbourhoods or shared needs and interests.[8] Many of these occupy the space described as the 'social and solidarity economy', employing more than five million people and with 123 million participating members across the European Union.[9] Partnerships are often formed between public bodies and NGOs for the purpose of delivering services.

The type, size and structure of an organization may determine how far its own purpose is aligned with the public interest and how well it is equipped to bid for government contracts, handle money, plan for the future, invest in improvement, recruit, train and retain staff, and give them decent pay and conditions, and how likely it is to share control with people who use services.

Some types of organization, notably large corporations and other for-profit companies, have values and motivations that are out of tune with the purpose of exercising collective responsibility to meet shared needs. Julie Froud and her colleagues at the Manchester School take the view that without strong regulation based on public values, fund investors and shareholders 'will have no inhibitions about using the devices of extraction and exploitation'.[10] They propose that all organizations, including private companies, that contract with government to provide goods and services to the public should have public status and explicitly share the same set of public interest goals, including 'equality, participation, quality of service, accountability, transparency, solidarity and public ethos'.

Funding arrangements

Arrangements for resourcing services vary across the range of ownership models and power relations. Major public services are fully funded through taxation, with levels of funding determined by government policy. In many cases, government bodies fully fund contracted-out services; they also give grants to third-sector organizations to enable them to undertake various activities, often expecting them to raise further funds elsewhere, which may prove difficult or impossible. Businesses sometimes invest, but only where they anticipate comfortable returns. Philanthropic giving is an increasingly important source of funds as public expenditures are cut. Voluntary activity (unpaid labour) also provides substantial – and routinely undervalued – resources.[11]

Service users often have to make a financial contribution, and the level may be means-tested. In some cases public funds are distributed to individuals as direct payments or vouchers, which can be used to buy what they need or want (and can afford).[12]

Degrees of participation

Over the last two decades, it has become quite common for public authorities to engage local residents and groups of service users in discussions about how to plan the services they fund. Opinion surveys, focus groups, citizens' panels, community forums and deliberative workshops have come to feature regularly in the dealings of local authorities and other funding bodies. Some engagement exercises have managed to improve the scope and quality of services and to strengthen local support for them. Some have helped to ease the pain of service cuts and build alliances between voluntary and publicly funded organizations. Others have just made people fed up and cynical because their participation has made no perceptible difference. Much depends on how engagement is organized, how far power shifts towards residents and service users, how genuinely their views are sought and heeded, and how results feed through to decisions and action.

There has been a similar trend among non-government service providers, many of whom now have policies that support user participation and 'personalization' – an approach that aims to tailor services to individuals' specific needs and circumstances. The extent to which people actually participate in decisions about services varies widely, from receiving information and being consulted, to being actively engaged and co-producing services at the planning, design and delivery stages. Co-production involves users and providers of services forming an equal partnership and combining lay and expert knowledge to develop ways of meeting needs. Advocates of 'commoning' envisage people taking control of identifying needs and the best way to meet them, as well as design and delivery. Co-production and commoning challenge the very idea of a 'service' because they focus on people being part of the action to meet their own needs, rather than simply having services delivered to them – hence our reference to 'activities' rather than just services in our opening definition of UBS.[13]

Effective participation calls for profound changes in the way professionals and other service workers think, act and interact with others. They need new skills, according to David Boyle and others who have led the move towards co-production: 'These include being able to see and harness the assets that people have, to make room for people to develop for themselves, and to use a wide variety of methods for working with people rather than processing them'. It entails a change of focus 'away from a culture of "caring for" to a culture of enabling and facilitating, but the skill-set must also be able to change systems and operate on a large scale'.[14]

One leading UK expert in public participation observes that austerity has been a 'poor bedfellow' of participation, as policy makers pay lip service to the idea while implementing spending cuts that make genuine participation possible. 'Retreat from meaningful involvement impoverishes public provision, undermines accountability and creates a vicious circle of ever-diminishing engagement and support.'[15]

How Would It Work in Practice?

Conditionality

The universal component of UBS is access for all according to need, not ability to pay. Rather obviously, you are not expected to receive a service such as housing or child care if you don't need it (this is one of several ways in which UBS is different from UBI, where everyone is supposed to get regular cash payments, whether they need them or not). Who decides who needs what will vary from one area of need to another: eligibility may depend on professional judgement, locality or age, or on a claim by the individual – or a combination of these. It should be the role of the state to ensure that access is equitable as well as secure.

Assuming universality is country specific rather than global, who within a nation would be eligible for access to services to meet their needs? Would eligibility derive from citizenship or from residence, or something else? Leading economist Tony Atkinson put forward the idea of entitlement based on resident participation.[16] This could be broadly defined as making a social contribution – for example, by full or part-time waged employment or self-employment, by education, training or active job search, by home care for children or the elderly or disabled, or by regular voluntary work in a recognized association, or a portfolio of activities equalling around 35 hours per week.[17] It has been described as 'a move towards a reimagined social citizenship, based on plural identities and rights conferred on residents rather than on passport-holders'.[18]

Entitlements

This proposal can only be realized through a range of entitlements shared by all who are eligible. In generic terms, these include 'negative' rights or freedoms, such as the right to protection from unfair treatment on grounds of gender or ethnicity, as well as political rights to participate in decisions about shaping and allocating services and benefits. These are typically established in law, although often limited in practice.

At the same time, crucially, UBS would embrace 'positive' social rights to services and resources. These are strongly linked with the vision of social citizenship that underpins post-war welfare states. They enable people to claim the means that are essential for participating fully in society and for realizing their civil and political rights. They feature in the constitutions of some countries. For example, Finland's constitution 'guarantees economic, social and cultural (ESC) rights', such as the right to work, education, indispensable subsistence and care, social security and adequate social, health and medical services, which the authorities are required to guarantee and promote.[19] The Belgian constitution declares that 'Everyone has the right to lead a life in keeping with human dignity' and binds most laws and regulations to 'guarantee economic, social and cultural rights', which include fair employment and pay, health care, housing, social security, the protection of a healthy environment and the right to cultural and social fulfilment.[20]

There is often quite a distance between what is written in a constitution and what happens in practice, but declarations of this kind set out what is *agreed to be desirable*. At best, they can serve as a touchstone and support for progressive policy makers, local initiatives and social movements, and to reinforce political action.

Most declarations of social rights need further development, including legislation, to put them into practice. For social rights to be realized, they should ideally be codified in law and be accompanied by a robust framework of 'procedural rights', that is, systems and protocols that enable people to know and claim what they are entitled to by means that are fair, accessible, timely and affordable.[21] Social rights would of course require political support. They would have to be established and upheld through institutions of the state, which would also have to ensure that corresponding duties and duty-bearers were identified and suitably resourced and supported to fulfil their duties.

The role of the state

The quality and scope of UBS depend on how all these variables are combined in each case and how they interact. We envisage a landscape where different kinds of organization, as well as different contracts and funding arrangements coexist and where services workers and people who use services play a variety of roles to suit different circumstances. Crucially, the state retains four key roles: to ensure equality of access, to set and enforce standards, to collect and invest funds, and to coordinate functions across sectors to maximize positive impacts.

This points to a new dynamic between 'bottom-up' and 'top-down' politics, and significant changes in the culture and practice of public authorities. Government officials should see it as their role to encourage inclusive participation and local control, welcome innovation, facilitate diverse activities, actively support the efforts of local organizations to meet quality standards (instead of just policing them), and invest adequate resources equitably between different groups and localities. This is about changing whole systems, not making piecemeal reforms.

Common features

Taking all these complexities into account, we can see the need for a customized approach to UBS. Yet there are certain features that apply in all cases.

- Collective responsibility for meeting shared needs will be exercised through democratically elected governments.
- Power will be devolved to the lowest appropriate level (according to the principle of subsidiarity).
- Services will be delivered by a range of organizations with different models of ownership and control, all sharing a clear set of enforceable public interest obligations.
- They will be accessible and affordable for all, according to need, not ability to pay.
- There will be meaningful participation in designing and delivering services by residents and

service users, working in close partnership with professionals and other front-line workers.

- There will be clear rules and procedures for fair and inclusive eligibility and entitlement.
- The state will ensure equality of access, set and enforce standards, raise and invest funds, and coordinate functions between services.

3

The Benefits of UBS

UBS may be complex and challenging, but it offers benefits that range across four dimensions: equality, efficiency, solidarity and sustainability. Here, our analysis refers to existing services such as health care and schooling, and to the new services we map out in the following chapters. Collectively generated activities to meet other areas of need, provided they are well organized and supported, may have similar effects.

Equality

Public services reduce income inequalities by providing a social wage that is worth much more to people on the lowest incomes. A study of OECD countries found that poor people would have to spend three-quarters of their income on essential services such as health care and education if they had to purchase them directly. Services reduced income inequality by an average of 20%.[1] Modelling by the Institute for Global Prosperity found that extending public services to new areas, such as transport and access to digital information, would have far greater value, proportionately, to low-income households than to rich ones.[2]

Services bring benefits without which individuals and families would be unable to meet their needs and flourish. Getting an education makes it easier to find work and earn money; access to housing and health care means there is less risk of becoming disabled by illness and dependent on care; access to transport and the internet makes it possible to get work, avoid isolation, use other services, and so on. These things are especially important for low-income families because of the knock-on effects that shield them against accumulating risks and vulnerabilities.

The effects are not just individual: reducing inequalities will benefit society as a whole. As Wilkinson and Pickett have demonstrated, outcomes for a range of health and social problems (physical and mental health, drug abuse, education, imprisonment, obesity, social mobility, trust and community life, violence, teen pregnancies and child well-being) are significantly worse in more unequal rich countries.[3]

Some studies have suggested that public services are more likely to benefit those who are better off.[4] It is easy to understand that better-educated, more confident people may find it easier to navigate access to some services and get what they need. Yet, overall, there is strong evidence that public services benefit lower-income households disproportionately. A detailed analysis of the distributional effects of the social wage in the United Kingdom in 2002 confirmed a consistent pro-poor bias in most services, which had increased over two decades and continues to do so to this day.[5] Figure 3.1 shows the distribution of social wage value across income groups in the United Kingdom, with the lowest-income households receiving more in social wages than they do in cash incomes.

However, the extent and consistency of the redistributive effects depends on how universal services are designed, delivered and funded – as well as how they interact with each other.

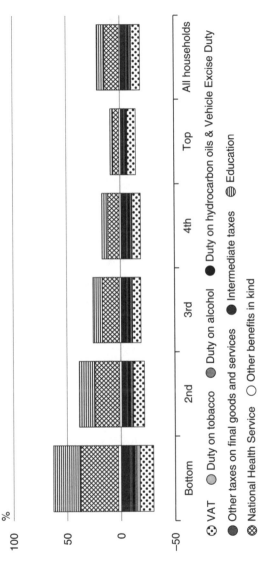

Figure 3.1 UK: Indirect taxes and benefits-in-kind as a proportion of disposable income by quintile groups, all households; financial year ending 2017

Source: Office for National Statistics

The Benefits of UBS

Efficiency

Efficiency is usually measured in terms of the ratio between inputs and outputs: the greater the amount of useful output per unit of input, the more efficient the process is deemed to be. In public policy, *inputs* can refer to expenditure of resources, such as money or labour, as well as government regulation. *Outputs* refer to the implementation of legislation and the delivery of specific transfers and services, such as social care or clinical procedures. *Outcomes* refer to the broader and longer-term impacts on individuals (such as poverty and mortality) or on social distributions (e.g. levels of inequality).[6] They will be influenced by how services interact with each other, as well as by a wide range of social, cultural and economic conditions. Given these complexities, measures of efficiency in the public sector are usually complex and contested.

Public services have often been accused of inefficiencies, which market theorists have attributed to lack of competition and the vested interests of bureaucrats and professions. These shortcomings have been used to justify introducing market rules into public services from the 1980s onwards. But competition between multiple providers, customer choice for service users and conventional cost-efficiency criteria for measuring success have largely failed to improve outputs, let alone outcomes. These failings have been greatly exacerbated by public-spending cuts, with decisions often predicated on the notion that simply reducing inputs is equivalent to increasing efficiency. Getting 'more for less' by cutting staff or increasing workload to compete in a quasi-marketplace has generally proved to be self-defeating.[7]

Market processes can deliver output inefficiencies in many public services. Private contracts tend to be inflexible and limit the ability of public authorities to improve services and respond to changing demands.[8] Transaction costs are often higher for both consumers and providers, not least because a for-profit system extracts funds to pay dividends to shareholders. Public sector organizations can keep costs down in ways that cannot be achieved by competing commercial organizations – for example, through sharing administrative, purchasing and research functions, by avoiding duplication and by working together to achieve shared goals.[9] Moral hazards are encountered when profit incentives combine with unequal knowledge in markets. For example, private medical providers may have profit-related incentives to undertake unnecessary medical interventions, while patients know too little to judge whether they are right or wrong.[10]

Turning to outcomes efficiency, there are further advantages to a public – rather than market-based – system in many service areas. Where collective activities are intended to serve the public interest, receive funding from public sources and share a democratic framework, they are, in theory at least, better able to interact in mutually beneficial ways – and they can be coordinated to do so by public authorities. One example is where schools encourage healthy eating and active pursuits, making children healthier; others are where bus services enable people to get to work or where high-quality child care helps children to get more out of primary education.

Definitive studies of the efficiency of public services are rare, and most that do exist focus on health care and cost-efficiency. A 2016 study compared spending on health care and average life expectancy in OECD countries. It found the United States, which is a mainly market-based system, outspent the United Kingdom in 2014 by the equivalent of £6,311 per person, compared with £2,777, yet had an average life expectancy at birth of 78.8 years, compared with 81.4 in the United Kingdom.[11]

Other studies have found that, while the United Kingdom spends a smaller proportion of GDP on health care than other European countries, the NHS is one of the more efficient and cost-effective health-care systems in the world.[12]

Where efficiency is assessed in narrow output terms, calculations overlook the multiple dimensions of value, the many ways in which value is experienced and how it accrues. The concept of 'social return on investment' (SROI) has been developed over the last decade and adopted by the UK government in the 2012 Social Value Act, which instructs public service commissioners to consider how to 'improve the social, economic and environmental well-being of the relevant area'.[13]

Applying social value analysis to assessing service efficiency means taking account of longer-term, indirect effects as well as short-term direct ones. This does not sit easily with a market-based system. For example, if staff delivering meals on wheels to people who are housebound take time to sit and chat with them, this may reduce their sense of social isolation and generally improve their well-being, but it will increase costs by demanding additional staff time. If a school opens up as a community centre at weekends, it may improve opportunities for local residents to get together and help each other in various ways with positive long-term effects, but it will also eat into the school budget. Some forms of social value take years to accumulate, with no immediate tangible benefits; often, they accrue in ways that do not return dividends of any kind to the organization that made the investment in the first place. Nevertheless they can yield substantial returns on investment over time, which are routinely overlooked because they are hard to measure, not because they lack value.

There is clearly a disconnect between conventional ways of assessing efficiency, on the one hand, and notions of value that are anchored in whole systems and human relationships, on the other. It has prompted many to challenge the dominance of economic growth as an indicator of national progress and the norms of cost-efficiency accounting. Some countries have begun to measure human well-being, alongside GDP (gross domestic product), as an indicator of national progress. Michel Bauwens, founder of the Peer-to-Peer Foundation (P2P), has called for a major 'value shift': instead of rewarding 'extractive' practices 'that enrich some at the expense of the others', we should reward 'generative' practices that enrich the social and environmental resources to which they are applied.[11] The efficiency of universal basic services may best be judged from this perspective – by how far they lead to outcomes that renew local assets, safeguard planetary boundaries and nurture human flourishing.

The Benefits of UBS

Solidarity

The concepts of shared needs and collective responsibilities embody the idea of solidarity, and the practice of UBS, as we have defined it, has potential to develop and strengthen solidarity. We take solidarity to mean feelings of sympathy and responsibility between people that promote mutual support. It is an inclusive process, not just within well-acquainted groups but also, crucially, between people and groups who are 'strangers' to each other. It involves collective action towards shared objectives.[15]

As a policy goal, UBS calls for collective policy and practice: sharing resources and acting together to deal with risks and problems that people cannot cope with alone. It is not something that can be achieved by individuals or groups simply fending for themselves and pursuing their own interests. As Durkheim observed, society is not constructed through atomized choices spontaneously generating cooperation but by mutual regard and consideration.[16]

The conviction is echoed in the European Union's long-standing goal of economic and social cohesion, by which it means combining a market economy with 'a commitment to the values of internal solidarity and mutual support which ensures open access for all members of society to services of general benefit and protection'.[17] Solidarity can be undermined by market interests, especially at times of crisis, but this commitment has underpinned major programmes to redistribute funds to disadvantaged areas and promote equalities across the European Union.

Pursuing the goal of more and better public services not only requires solidarity but also contributes to it – in three main ways. First, it develops experience of shared needs and collective responsibility, which builds understanding of how people depend on each other and a commitment to retaining these interconnections. Second, where services bring people together from different social groups, they can provide opportunities for developing mutual sympathy and responsibility. Third, the combined effects of more and better services, as we have noted, bring benefits to society as a whole and have a redistributive effect, reducing inequalities that otherwise create barriers to solidarity.

Some have argued that welfare states – and thereby public services – 'crowd out' social capital by inhibiting informal caring networks, mutual trust and social norms that favour civil commitment and trustworthiness. However, it is not the existence of public services that carries this risk but how they work – in whose interests, under whose control and with what outcomes. There is evidence that Nordic-style welfare regimes, where there are more universal services and a stronger collective ethos, tend to have higher, rather than lower, levels of bonding and bridging social capital.[18]

Much evidence and commentary relating to solidarity and public services focus on how 'calculations of individual self-interest diminish collective understanding and recognition of mutual need.'[19] Richard Titmuss famously demonstrated that a market-based blood donation service is likely to be less effective than a collective one based on voluntary donations.[20] In another much-cited case, nursery staff decided to fine parents who collected their children late, to encourage good timekeeping, but parents interpreted the fine as payment for services and felt able to 'buy themselves out of their social contract', defeating the object of the exercise.[21] There is a rich literature on the ways in which systems based on individualism, choice and competition weaken the values of social citizenship and undermine solidarity.[22]

The Benefits of UBS

Sustainability

Sustainability involves, at its simplest, an inherent 'capacity for continuance'.[23] That suggests a system that can function in ways that continue to achieve its desired goals over time. UBS could have positive impacts on sustainability through prevention of harm, through economic stabilization and through helping to mitigate climate change and the depletion of natural resources.

It is hard to overstate the importance of measures that address the upstream causes of social, economic and environmental harm. Failure to act cannot be justified on ethical or practical grounds because of the untold human misery and incalculable costs of dealing with crises and catastrophes when things go wrong. Preventative services not only help people to stay well and flourish; they can also reduce demand for a range of services, not just health care. Unemployment, anti-social behaviour and many forms of crime, for example, have roots in poverty and deprivation, which can be significantly reduced by a more generous 'social wage'.[?]

Yet, paradoxically, while everyone recognizes the potential benefits of prevention, it is rarely prioritized. Most public services operate in silos and remain predominantly 'downstream' operations,

47

addressing a variety of needs and harms that are avoidable. Measures of success, as we have noted, often overlook longer-term effects, or where investment from one department yields benefits to another. Reversing this focus will require a thorough overhaul of public policy. The two basic foundations of prevention are, first, a scientific understanding of cause and effect and the possibility of prediction and, second, a capacity for controlled government intervention in social life.[25] So, despite past failures, effective prevention will entail an enlarged and more integrated role for public intervention – of which UBS is a crucial component.

Where the economy is concerned, public services can help to stabilize fluctuations by generating relatively secure employment. While they are vulnerable to cuts in government spending, they are not directly linked to downturns in the market. This applies not only to public sector bodies, but to the many non-government organizations that – in our vision of UBS – are vehicles for collective action to meet shared needs. They can be seen as part of the 'social economy', which has been described as 'an engine for social innovation, solidarity and social investment', with incentive structures that tend to support employment solidarity.[26] When times get tough, workers are more willing to trade off higher pay for collective job security. Along with the public sector bodies with which they often work in partnership, they act as a counter-cyclical buffer, helping to offset the effects of market downturns and recession, contributing to the economy's 'capacity for continuance'.

The most profound threat to human flourishing is that of climate collapse and extreme environmental stress, as we have noted. The entire edifice of environmental sustainability is premised on prevention – or *mitigation* as it is called because some future heating of the planet cannot now be prevented. This provides strong justification for UBS.

A move towards more and better public services is likely to prove more environmentally sustainable than a market-based system. For a start, UBS can play a vital role in switching the entire economy from a fixation on economic growth to a concern for human well-being within planetary limits. Public provisioning systems are better able than market systems to promote sustainable consumption, to coordinate sustainable practices such as active travel (e.g. cycling, walking), resource-efficient buildings and local food procurement, and to implement national strategies for reducing GHG emissions. Where governments issue guidance, public sector organizations are more likely to comply because they share public interest values. Where public bodies work with non-government partners or sub-contractors, they can spread sustainable practices among a wider range of institutions.

There is some evidence that collectively provided services have a smaller ecological footprint than privately funded alternatives. For example, the US healthcare system directly accounts for 8% of emissions in the United States, compared with the UK system, where 3% of emissions directly stem from the NHS. This is due both to the greater macro-efficiency and lower expenditure shares of health care in the United Kingdom, and to lower emissions per pound or dollar spent, which is thought to be a result of better resource allocation and procurement practices.[27] There is also some evidence that more extensive welfare states are generally better suited to adopting and implementing pro-environmental policies, especially where they embody ideas about shared needs and collective responsibilities.[28]

Public services perform important precautionary environmental and climate functions in their own right. The impact of Hurricane Katrina on the predominantly poor and black populations of Louisiana (where more than 1,500 died), in contrast to its impact on Cuba (where only two died) demonstrated the importance of collective ethos and services in dealing with climate-related risks.

Finally, public services have a vital role to play in ensuring that sustainable policies are socially just. For example, programmes to retrofit the vast bulk of the housing stock, proposed for the United Kingdom as part of a Green New Deal, will require public planning, finance and management.[29] If government can coordinate the range of services effectively, they can offset any regressive effects of climate policies (such as higher energy prices) and ensure a 'just transition' to sustainable living.

Considering UBS alongside cash payments

As we noted at the start of this book, more and better public services should be combined with a more generous, less conditional and non-stigmatizing system of social security that gives everyone the right to a living income. This begs the question of how such a combination can best be achieved. While it is argued that public funds can be increased substantially, there is bound to be a trade-off between money devoted to cash payments and money devoted to public services. What matters is the level at which the budget for cash payments begins to divert funds that could otherwise be spent on improving and extending services.

Many leading advocates of cash payment schemes, described as universal basic income (UBI) or basic income (BI), call for regular, unconditional cash payments to every individual, regardless of income and status, with payments that are sufficient to live on at a basic level, or nearly so – and therefore set at or near the poverty line in any country. The International Labour Office (ILO) recently calculated the costs of a similarly defined cash-payment (UBI) system in 130 countries, and found that 'for most world regions, the average costs . . . are in the range of 20 to 30 per cent of GDP.'[30] This, in our view, would wildly exceed the threshold at which cash payments could be fiscally compatible with UBS.

Furthermore, cash distribution is not about exercising collective responsibility to meet shared needs but about making payments to individuals to help them to buy what they need (or want). A system that supports market-based consumption may not be best placed to address problems such as poverty, precarious employment and inequality, which themselves have emerged from free-market practices. Some champions of UBI/BI see cash payments as an alternative to public services and a route to recommodifying welfare states. More progressive advocates usually acknowledge that cash payments should be underpinned by a strong framework of public services, but nowhere do they explain how both could be sufficient and affordable at the same time – let alone how sufficient payments could be funded alongside an ambitious programme to improve and extend the social wage.

There is no room here for a detailed discussion of UBI or BI. But it is worth reflecting briefly on how the approach to cash payments envisaged by protagonists (summarized above) compares with UBS across the four dimensions of equality, efficiency, solidarity and sustainability. There are many different versions and meanings attached to each descriptor and they are often used interchangeably. For the sake of simplicity, we use 'UBI' throughout the following paragraphs.

Equality

If you give cash payments to people who have little or nothing, it is bound to make at least a small improvement in their lives. But cash payments on their own cannot reduce inequalities. As the ILO observes, this can never amount to 'a stand-alone solution to redress an ever more unequal primary distribution of incomes'. People need power and access to a range of social and material resources that cash payments could not enable them to buy. Without a coherent policy framework that takes these broader factors into account, says the ILO, 'a UBI may exacerbate inequality'.[31] There is simply no conceivable scenario where funding a sufficient UBI scheme would be compatible with funding the full range of public provision needed to achieve social justice rather than minimal poverty relief. If the balance of investment in any country were to swing away from services towards cash payments, the value of the social wage would fall, hitting the poor hardest.

Efficiency

If a UBI scheme replaced all means-tested benefits, it could arguably simplify and reduce the administrative costs of income support. But, as most UBI protagonists admit, it would need to be topped up by some conditional payments – for example, for people with physical or mental disabilities. At the same time, the tax system would have to be overhauled to claw back part or all of the payments for people on higher incomes. One critic, envisaging a small and affordable UBI, describes a 'powerful new tax engine [that] will pull along a tiny cart'.[32] It is hard to see how this would be more efficient than the status quo. Certainly, cash transfers should not be increased without a proper assessment of whether the same goals could be achieved more effectively through public services.

If a UBI scheme were to replace public services as well as income support, people would be left to buy themselves out of any trouble that happened to befall them. As we have noted, market-based systems are less efficient than collective services for meeting many of our shared needs because of higher transaction costs, greater risk of moral hazard and the pursuit of profit. Efforts to generate value through a UBI scheme and return it to the source of input (the people who receive and spend the cash payments) will very likely be outweighed by extractive practices in the marketplace.

Solidarity

Giving money to individuals to spend as they wish does nothing to bring them together or build a sense of common purpose. On the contrary, it plugs them into a market system that feeds on choice and competition. It erodes the relational base of services and the ethos of shared interest and collective responsibility. In the words of Francine Mestrum, the radical Belgian writer and analyst, basic income is an individualist solution to a set of shared problems:

'progressives will look for other solutions, based on solidarity, reciprocity and collective action'.[33]

Sustainability

Ed Whitfield, founder of the US-based Fund for Democratic Communities, argues that a guaranteed basic income would 'only help people have more access to consumption without altering anything about how production is organised.'[34] Such a scheme can do nothing to change patterns of consumption, to encourage more sustainable use of resources, or to create the conditions for collective approaches to climate mitigation at local or national levels. Cash payments may prevent starvation, but they have nothing to offer that is strategically preventative over time, nothing to build the 'capacity for continuance' in social, economic or environmental terms.

In summary, we don't see UBS as a natural policy companion to a UBI scheme of sufficient cash payments to all. This is because the two conflict ideologically and could not both be affordable and sufficient at the same time. On grounds of equality, efficiency, solidarity and sustainability, there is a strong case for giving priority to UBS and seeking more compatible ways of reforming social security systems.

4

Rolling Out UBS: Meeting Needs for Care

Health care and schooling are services where the principles of UBS (exercising collective responsibility to meet shared needs) are already applied in most rich countries – albeit in different ways and often imperfectly. In this chapter, we focus on how the principles could be applied in other areas of need. But there are important lessons to be learned from health care and schooling. Here are just two.

The first, which comes mainly from the NHS, is a continuing failure to focus on the underlying causes of ill health. It is health, after all, that is our basic need, and health care is only one way of meeting it. Most long-term health conditions (such as diabetes, many cancers, pulmonary and heart disease) are avoidable and yet they are the main source of pressure on the service. There is no shortage of evidence about their causes and what can be done to prevent them, most of which falls well beyond the remit of the NHS (housing, education, diet, exercise, air quality, employment conditions, poverty and powerlessness). This calls for a far stronger policy focus, backed up by resources, on coordinating services and other collective activities beyond the NHS that prevent illness and help people to stay well. The aim should be a healthier population, not a bigger health service.

The second, which comes mainly from the education sector, is the danger of elevating choice and competition above collective responsibility. Education is an important determinant of health and provides a crucial underpinning for meeting all our shared needs. It should be available to all in equal measure. This is not about uniformity but about everyone having equal access to education of a comparable standard, so that no one is left behind. This calls into question the validity of public subsidies (in the form of tax breaks for registered charities) to fee-paying schools; the proliferation of academies and so-called 'free' schools operating beyond local democratic control; and admissions criteria and catchment areas that separate pupils by class, religion and ethnicity. If UBS means exercising collective responsibility for meeting shared needs, the preferences (or wants) of some parents should not make it more difficult to meet the needs of others.

Rolling out the UBS agenda must include radical improvements in health care, schooling and other services, such as policing, which are already (in theory if not always in practice) free and universal. Beyond that, our aim is to reach into new areas where there are unmet needs that call for a collective response. We turn now to child care and adult social care, where there are some free services in many countries but seldom enough to meet everyone's needs sufficiently. In the following chapter, we consider how the approach can be extended beyond the care sector to housing, transport and access to digital information.

Remember, there is no single formula for this. Each service should be accessible to all according to need not ability to pay. In some cases, we propose that services are free to all at the point of use. In others, the critical factor may be a realizable entitlement to the service, rather than free provision: here, we envisage a strong element of collective funding, combined with low-cost charges for users and partial or total exemptions to ensure that they are genuinely affordable to all. It may not be ideal – not least because of well-known problems associated with means testing. But we want to be pragmatic as well as radical. We have tried to take account of the distinctive nature of each area of need and how it can be satisfied, as well as the history and politics of provision, building as far as possible on models that have been tested in practice.

Child care

Education, security in childhood and work are among the generic needs 'satisfiers' we listed in the first chapter. Child care[1] can deliver on all of these: early education and care for pre-school-age children, plus enabling parents to go out to work. It is a shared need that can only be met for all by exercising collective responsibility. Poor children and families have more to gain from it – and are more disadvantaged without it – than those who are better off. [2] That puts it squarely in the range of UBS.

Many countries have well-developed childcare systems. Some, such as the United Kingdom, were initially driven by wanting more women in the labour force; others, such as the United States, aimed primarily to compensate for childhood disadvantage. Norway has a long-standing pedagogical tradition that values early education and care for pre-school children. New Zealand (between 1999 and 2008) developed policy on early childhood education as 'a broad and holistic concept that covers children, families and communities', which was recognized as 'investing in infrastructure, just like building roads'.[3] The challenge in almost every country is to ensure that a sufficiently high quality of child care is universally accessible.

Balancing quality, quantity and affordability
Factors that contribute to quality in child care include training and qualifications of staff, ratios of children to staff (lower is generally better), a good mix between children with different social and ethnic backgrounds, suitably warm, consistent relationships between children and staff, parental involvement in managing childcare centres and opening times to suit parents' working lives.

Norway, which sets an enviable example in most aspects of child care, has well-qualified staff, relatively high staff–child ratios, a consistent form of childcare setting (the kindergarten) and continuity of care from age one to six as the norm. It combines 'a legal guarantee to a place for all children with fees that are both low overall and income-related'.

In most countries, child care is provided by a mix

of for-profit, public and voluntary organizations. The role of for-profit providers has a bearing on both cost and quality because resources are likely to be 'siphoned off for shareholders rather than invested in staff wages and other quality inputs'.[4] Where for-profit provision is combined with a demand-led, fee-paying system, the observed effects are 'a rise in the fees charged by providers, a drop in standards in poorer areas, and an increase in inequalities of access'.[5] But Norway has reportedly managed to expand provision, open it up to private businesses and still maintain quality. This is attributed to the fact that government covers 85% of childcare costs, caps fees, imposes tight regulations on staff qualifications, limits profit to what is 'reasonable' and ensures that parents sit on kindergarten boards.

To make sure children from disadvantaged backgrounds participate, research suggests that 'the most effective strategy is universal access plus outreach to vulnerable groups, not one or the other'.[6] An exhaustive study of child care in OECD countries (Australia, France, Germany, the Netherlands, New Zealand, the United States and the United Kingdom) concluded that 'free and universal services have much higher enrolment rates than services with a fee' and are the best way of reaching disadvantaged families; where there are fees, even if they are low, they are more likely to deter access than free provision.[7]

However, entirely free universal high-quality child care for all pre-school children is bound to be expensive, and few governments have been willing to make the necessary investment, in spite of strong evidence about the benefits it can bring. In Denmark, which is typical of more generous state funders, local authorities are expected to cover no less than 75% of costs, while parents pay no more than 25%. For a lone parent in the United States, childcare costs are over half of net income, and in Ireland that figure is 42%. Couples in the United Kingdom and New Zealand spend around a third of their income on child care.[8]

Some governments struggle to provide a sufficient quantity or quality of child care, especially where it is supposed to be an entitlement. In the United Kingdom, three- and four-year-olds are entitled to up to 30 hours of free child care a week, while some two-year-olds in low income families get 15 hours of free child care. Government subsidies are supposed to offset the costs, but in many areas the actual costs of providing care outstrip the subsidy. Providers have cut qualified staff, shortened opening hours or restricted places to keep costs down.

One-third of local authorities in England, 40% in Wales and 14% in Scotland do not have enough early education for three- and four-year-olds eligible for universal free entitlements.[9] Where it is available it can be prohibitively expensive and discourage parents, particularly women, from going out to work.[10]

Public spending on child care

Total public spending on child care (including care, pre-school education and related in-kind benefits) as a percentage of gross domestic product (GDP) ranges from 1.66% in France, 1.45% in Norway and 1.39% in the Netherlands to 1.13% in the United Kingdom, 0.75% in Germany and 0.65% in Australia, leaving the United States at the lower end with spending worth 0.55% of GDP.[11]

Spending and quality are inevitably intertwined. In the United Kingdom, campaigners have argued that in order to achieve high-quality care, childcare workers should have training and salaries comparable to primary school staff. They have calculated, accordingly, that free universal provision for children aged six months to the start of compulsory schooling would produce gross costs representing 3% of GDP. They also estimate that nine-tenths of the costs would be recouped through employment gains, increased tax revenues and reduced income support payments.[12]

Returns on investment

Once child care is regarded as an investment ('just like building roads'), the benefits far outweigh the costs. Accessible, affordable, high-quality child care enables parents – especially women and lone parents – to enter and stay in paid employment. The point here is not that all parents should get a job, whether they want to or not, but that paid work can be a route to financial independence, especially for women, and lack of child care often exacerbates gender inequalities in pay and job opportunities. Child care helps children do better at school and to flourish long after they have left school. Children with experience of pre-school education and care are less likely to be unemployed or to get in trouble with the law. The OECD has identified a range of social benefits that can be derived from 'high quality early childhood education and care', including better health, reduced likelihood of individuals engaging in risky behaviour and stronger 'civic and social engagement', with positive 'spill-over effects' for society as a whole.[13] In other words, child care is a preventative measure, helping to avoid various kinds of harm that would otherwise impair people's well-being and call for costly interventions by a range of public agencies.

A UK study using social return on investment (SROI) analysis found that investment in a combination of universal child care, targeted interventions for disadvantaged children and paid parental leave could reduce government spending on 'social problems such as crime, mental ill health, family breakdown, drug abuse and obesity'. Every £1 spent in a centre providing free child care was thereby expected to generate a 'return to society of £4.60'.[14] Such calculations are only indicative, but they help to shed light on the longer-term, indirect effects of investment that are too often overlooked.

In summary

Child care is an obvious candidate for inclusion in the UBS agenda. Providing free, or at least genuinely affordable, childcare services for all children between the end of parental leave and the start of compulsory schooling would be a sensible investment, yielding substantial social and economic returns – more than enough to justify the expenditure. But only services of a sufficient quality that are customized to suit different conditions and social groups and sustained over time will produce such results.

Adult social care

Adults who are disabled, frail or vulnerable need care from others. This is essential if they are to maintain their health, autonomy and capacity for social participation. Close relatives often provide the necessary care, but in many cases they cannot do so – either because they lack the skills or resources or because it impairs their capacity to meet their own needs. On these grounds, secure, good-quality adult social care should be a universal basic service.

Preventing need

Numbers needing adult social care are growing rapidly. In the United Kingdom, around 3.5 million older people currently need care, with numbers projected to rise to 5.9 million by 2040.[15] This is usually attributed – uncritically – to the fact that people are living longer, many with multiple chronic conditions that intensify with age. There is an alarming lack of policy focus on what can be done earlier in life to prevent age-related conditions that trigger need for care. We all die in the end, obviously, but what matters is how long we can remain well and independent. There is no shortage of evidence that most long-term illnesses are avoidable.[16]

So it is not enough to call for more and better

adult social care services. The starting premise should be that older people are an asset to society, rather than a problem. We must think in terms of a whole system in which care for those who are unable to look after themselves is combined with collective activities that maintain and improve well-being across the life cycle. These would include the range of services included in the UBS agenda, as well as specific measures such as access to physical exercise, opportunities to socialize, a flexible approach to retirement and lifelong learning.

If prevention were taken seriously and acted upon, there would be no reason to assume that care needs and costs will rise in matching step with population ageing. Nevertheless, it is important to pay attention to how adult social care can be available for all who need it, regardless of ability to pay.

Balancing quality, quantity and affordability
As with all services in the UBS agenda, the goal is to ensure that everyone who needs it can gain access to a sufficiently high quality of service. The starting point is entitlement: everyone has a right to the care they need. There is then a balance to be struck between quality, quantity and affordability. In the field of adult social care, there are six crucial factors affecting this balancing act. The first,

already noted, is the extent to which measures are in place to prevent care needs arising. The second is informal care (the unpaid labour of predominantly family members) and how well it relates to and is valued and supported by formal care systems. The third factor is the paid workforce: their training, qualifications, pay and working conditions. Fourth, there is participation by people who need care and their informal carers – how far they are involved in finding solutions to their own care needs, and how far care is designed around the individual concerned ('personalization' in the jargon). Next, there is government regulation – to set and enforce standards of care, and to constrain (or eliminate) profiteering by commercial providers. Finally, there is the overarching factor of political choice, which can make or break all the others: whether to exercise collective responsibility to meet shared needs or to let the burden fall on individuals and their families.

How services are provided

What people need is highly individualized and varied over long periods of time. Services include home-based care, day centres and full-time residential care. Overall, adult social care depends heavily on a huge cohort of informal carers who work unpaid to look after their relatives and loved ones.

Around 6.5 million carers in the United Kingdom provide care whose value has been estimated at between £57 and £100 billion a year.[17] Informal carers need support, too. How much they get varies widely between countries. Denmark, Sweden, Norway, Finland and Iceland offer near-universal and comprehensive long-term support for carers, including long-term leave, cash benefits and benefits in kind.[18]

In most countries, care services are provided by a mix of public, non-profit and commercial organizations, with for-profit companies rapidly growing their share of the market. Some private firms manage to make large profits, often thanks to government contracts – although public spending cuts have squeezed the profitability of contracted-out services. Concerns have been raised in the United Kingdom about financialization in the care sector, where private equity firms rush to acquire businesses that seem to promise rich returns, then run up debts that lead to closures.[19]

Paying for care

Public spending on long-term care across OECD countries ranges from 4.3% of GDP in the Netherlands and 3.2% in Sweden, to 1.8% in France and 1.2% in the United Kingdom, with the

United States at 0.5% and Greece at zero.[20] This reflects different expectations about the balance of formal and informal care, and about how much people should pay out of their own pockets.

Options for paying for care include direct funding through taxation, payment via a contributory social insurance scheme to which employers and governments may also contribute, private insurance purchased by individuals, or direct payments by individual users which may (or may not) be partly or wholly offset by insurance or cash payments from government. There is usually a distinction between care and accommodation costs and it is common for individuals to have to cover the latter themselves. There is also a distinction between personal and medical care, with the latter more often covered by taxation or social insurance. In the United Kingdom, health care is almost invariably free, but poorly coordinated with a different funding system for long-term social care, the cost of which is estimated to rise from 1.1% to 2% of GDP over the coming decades.[21] In other countries, where health care is covered by social insurance, it is more common for long-term care to be included in the scheme.

The Netherlands was the first to introduce a universal system of long-term care insurance in 1968.

Sweden established the right to tax-funded social care in 1982/3. Compulsory long-term care insurance schemes were introduced in Germany in 1995, Japan in 2000, France in 2002 and Korea in 2008.[22] All these have provided at least some support to everyone with needs above a certain level, regardless of ability to pay. However, many governments have since struggled to maintain financial viability and have adopted various strategies to constrain costs. These include restricting services, raising contributions and introducing competition between insurers and/or providers.

In Scotland, personal care is free if you are over 65 and nursing care is free at any age, provided you are assessed and found to need care by your local authority.[23] In the rest of the United Kingdom, you have to meet the full costs if your capital is worth more than £23,250 a year (around 80% of median household income); if you have capital worth less than £14,250, you qualify for free care and in between you may get a partial subsidy.[24] All but the rich struggle to get the care they need. Lower- and middle-income families, except the very poor, can forfeit all their life savings and property values to pay for care. And free care for the poor is very often a poor service. Workers are put under increasing pressure to do more for less. Providers make profits even when standards of care are unacceptably low. As one care-related charity put it: 'We have seen company after company making millions whilst on the frontline vulnerable people are left without the basics to sustain life. Care staff are paid a pittance and asked to do the impossible with too few staff every day.[25]

Germany offers a more hopeful alternative. It has a long-term care insurance (LTCI) scheme featuring universal social rights within a strong cost-containment framework. The overall budget, contribution rates, ceilings, benefit levels and eligibility criteria are all fixed by federal law. For those in work, employers pay half the premium, while the retired pay full contributions, thus helping to address inter-generational equity concerns. LTCI membership is compulsory, and non-employed people are covered by employed householder insurance contributions. The scheme acknowledges that long-term care is a social risk requiring social protection and has cross-party political support. After 25 years of operation, despite population ageing, an extension of the scope of LTCI and increases in benefit levels, contributions have only increased by 0.8% of salaries.[26]

Returns on investment

Adult social care is as much part of the 'social infra-structure' as child care. Good quality care services can improve the well-being of elderly and vulnerable people and their carers; they can help some family members who would otherwise be trapped at home to take paid work; they can enrich local communities by enabling more people to participate; they can prevent or delay conditions getting worse and needing more intensive interventions; they can help to reduce demand for costly medical care. They can also provide secure, rewarding paid work for professional carers and others employed in the care sector, with multiplier effects for the economy.[27]

In summary

There is a strong ethical case for looking after disabled, frail and vulnerable members of society. A well-designed and sustainably resourced system should prevent need arising for as long as possible, support informal carers as well as the paid workforce, enforce high standards, crack down on profiteering and integrate funding for health and social care. This would provide a range of benefits that amply justify collective investment in long-term care.

5

Rolling Out UBS: Housing, Transport, Information

Now we move from the care sector to areas where goods and services – the 'material' and 'providential' infrastructure – are more closely intertwined. In housing, transport and information, there are distinctive systems of provision, combining material production and service delivery, historically shaped by technology, enterprise and competition, while the care sector has been shaped more by shared interests, family relationships and collective endeavour. We start in each of these with a different set of building blocks and different assumptions about how services are paid for and how to ensure that everyone gets what they need.

Housing

Everyone needs shelter. In a modern democracy, this implies more than a roof over one's head: we all need a place that is secure and supports our needs for health, autonomy and social participation. Patterns of ownership, control, quality and cost in housing can exert a powerful influence over the extent of social and economic well-being and inequalities in any country. They certainly do in the United Kingdom, where people with low incomes are far too often trapped in poor housing (if they are not homeless), where low-quality housing can also trap people in poverty, where rising house prices shape public attitudes and political priorities, and where a highly financialized property market severely distorts the national economy.

Housing is thus a prime candidate for inclusion in the UBS agenda. Applying the principles of UBS doesn't mean giving everyone a free dwelling. It does mean making sure there is a home for everyone that is secure, sufficient and affordable.

Housing as a universal basic service is more complicated than care, education or even transport. Essentially it consists of material goods – the bricks and mortar – that yield a stream of services over a prolonged period of time. No one except the very rich can afford to pay for a dwelling outright, and usually the cost of housing is spread out through rents or mortgage payments. Rents are most often paid to private or sometimes to 'social' landlords, the latter being government authorities or non-profit associations that operate under public interest obligations. New housing can be funded by government, by for-profit corporations and financial institutions, by non-profit and philanthropic organizations, or by partnerships formed between the various players, where power may or may not be exercised in the public interest. The challenge is to wrestle out of these and other complexities (such as location, land values and planning regimes) a set of arrangements that amount to a universal basic service.

First, a cautionary tale about the United Kingdom's severe and escalating housing crisis. It can be traced to the right-to-buy policies of the 1980s, which enabled council tenants to buy their homes at bargain prices (often then sold on or let out profitably) and, ever since, to the steady withdrawal of collective responsibility by government. For much of the mid-twentieth century the government took responsibility for delivering a sufficient supply of affordable homes for low- and middle-income tenants, but this is no longer the case, and now there are 1.2 million households on the waiting list for social housing in the United Kingdom. Owner occupation has become the housing status of choice. Nearly two-thirds of all dwellings (15.1million) are owner occupied; of the rest, 4.8 million are rented from private landlords, 2.4 million from housing associations and 1.4 from local authorities.[1]

Private developers and landlords have been allowed to dominate the market. Governments have failed to invest adequately in new building or to protect the interests of tenants. In London and other prime locations, rents and house prices have soared. For owner-occupiers, landlords, developers and banks, housing has become a financial asset, managed variously for individual security, family enrichment and corporate accumulation, rather than for meeting everyone's basic needs.

Social housing has been transformed into a residual 'ambulance service' for the least well off, as opposed to a mainstream tenure. There is technically a duty on local authorities to house the homeless, but most authorities have insufficient power or money to fulfil the duty adequately, and rough sleeping is increasingly familiar in towns and cities across the country. This pitiful landscape highlights the urgency of the case for UBS. Some other countries have done things differently and offer better prospects.

Security

Our starting point is individual entitlement to housing as one of life's necessities – a means for meeting one's basic needs. This is a matter for government legislation to establish positive social rights as well as procedural rights, as we have noted. There is a corresponding duty to enforce the entitlement, which is a matter of collective responsibility. In whatever tenure of housing people live – social, privately rented or owner occupied – they should be able to depend on the fact that they can reside without fear of eviction, provided they meet their obligations. The responsible body, typically a local authority, must have appropriate policies, as well as adequate capacity (powers and resources), which often depend on local or national government.

Beyond entitlement, security rests on how much control residents themselves have over their homes and neighbourhoods. Being allocated to damp, cramped accommodation in a run-down estate is not much of an entitlement. The rights of individuals, the politics and capacity of bodies exercising collective responsibility and the extent of residents' control are all intertwined to create the conditions for housing security.

Sufficiency

What constitutes 'sufficient' housing covers three main dimensions: the quality of the dwelling; the characteristics of the neighbourhood; and the extent to which residents have control over their housing and its surroundings.

How far a dwelling is sufficient is partly a matter of objective measures such as floor space per capita, fittings, outdoor space and amenities; it is also determined by subjective judgements shaped by history and culture. For example, home ownership is highly desirable in the United Kingdom, but in Vienna 80% of the population rent their homes, and more than half pay social rents. The Dutch and British prefer low-rise homes, while in many European cities, people in all income groups are content to live in high-rise apartments.

Residents' views about sufficiency will also be influenced by the quality of their surroundings, relationships with neighbours and how easily they can find their way to transport, jobs, schools, public services, shops, leisure facilities and open spaces. All these things can spell the difference between a living environment that enables people to meet their needs, and one that is experienced as inadequate or debilitating, making life a struggle.

The quality of housing and surroundings will

affect the mix of residents and ultimately shape the character of the neighbourhood. Ghettos of deprivation may be common in the United Kingdom, as are 'poor-door' social housing allocations in some private developments, where social tenants have separate entrances from the wealthier owner-occupiers. But elsewhere municipal authorities have set out to integrate residents from different backgrounds. Vienna has its Wohnfonds Wien policy that ensures mixed tenure of housing blocks, with the explicit aim of maintaining a social balance across the city. Singapore, too, has actively encouraged mixed-income neighbourhoods. In the new town of Ørestad near Copenhagen, social and private housing have been developed side by side, sharing enviable transport links, shops and amenities. Neighbourhoods where people from different backgrounds live side by side are more likely to generate mutual understanding and respect and a sense of shared responsibility for the community as a whole.

Sufficiency depends also on how residents participate in design and management. People tend to be healthier and happier if they have some control over their day-to-day living conditions.[2] This can range from being consulted as part of a residents' association, to co-producing decisions with landlords, to joining cooperative structures for owning and managing local housing. Housing co-ops flourish in many countries, including Austria, Denmark, Germany, Spain and Switzerland, where they run a considerable chunk of the housing stock. In parts of Copenhagen, up to 40% of housing units are owned and managed as cooperatives.[3] Where co-ops are at their best, there is firm and enduring political and practical support from government.

Sustainability

Closely bound up with both sufficiency and security is the imperative for housing to be sustainable: sufficiency within planetary boundaries and security for generations to come. This is reflected in the 'Green New Deal' proposal put to the US Congress in 2019, which calls for all new and upgraded buildings in the United States 'to achieve maximum energy efficiency, water efficiency, safety, affordability, comfort, and durability, including through electrification'. Notably, the US Green New Deal is about social justice and democracy as much as the environment: sustainable housing means not only designing and building zero-carbon homes using renewable resources but also developing neighbourhoods where everyone is encouraged to think and act sustainably.

The town of Freiburg in south-west Germany is claimed to be the 'solar capital of Europe' but that involves 'far more than simple technological conversion'. The Freiburg model reportedly promotes 'urban eco-living, facilitated by a strong long-term vision, national policy frameworks and a focused commitment to change and community engagement'.[4] There are many other developments across the world – although still far too few – that adopt similar approaches to sustainable housing.

Affordability

In a universal service, no one is excluded for want of money. Scarcity drives up prices, so increasing supply is an early goal wherever there are housing shortages – a common experience in cities across the world. Supply can be increased by building more dwellings, but it may be equally important to refurbish and redistribute existing stock, using regulation, taxation or compulsory purchase to discourage or eliminate empty dwellings and multiple home ownership.[5]

Allowing quality to fall victim to quantity would be counterproductive, so measures for boosting the supply side must also ensure sufficiency in the terms we have described. Markets are unlikely to produce sufficient and affordable housing unless they are shaped and managed by local and national government, using regulation, public investment and partnerships between commercial, state and other non-profit bodies. Public Asset Corporations in Copenhagen and Hamburg, and Montpellier's Special Purpose Vehicles for pooling and developing land are examples.

The cost of supplying more homes can be kept in check by investing public funds in infrastructure, land acquisition, building and retrofitting, by legislating to prevent speculation on land and property values, and by limiting profits extracted by private developers. Public funds can be raised by issuing government bonds, by taxing land and property as well as income, by generating revenue from local shops and amenities and by reinvesting revenues from rent and sales. There is also a case for taking land into collective ownership through municipal authorities or civil society vehicles such as community land trusts, so that it becomes a shared asset managed in the public interest, rather than a barrier to affordable housing.

The United Kingdom's Institute for Global Prosperity has proposed issuing 30-year government bonds to finance building 1.5 million new units to double the size of the social housing stock,[6] at a cost of 0.5% of GDP. In Vienna, the city government has kept housing affordable by owning most of the land, using municipal developments and supply-side subsidies to keep costs down. Denmark levies a tax on land, based on one-thousandth of the market value of the land, reviewed every two years, which is collected nationally and distributed to local government for reinvestment in housing and infrastructure. In England and Wales, a growing network of community land trusts, set up by local people, develop and manage affordable housing and other local assets. There are countless initiatives in cities across Europe that aim in these and other ways to boost the supply of affordable housing.[7]

Affordability is of course a relative notion, and even the least expensive homes are beyond the means of some. Poorer households generally pay a much larger slice of their income in rents or mortgages.[8] So further measures are needed if housing is to be genuinely affordable for all. These may take the form of demand-side benefits, such as housing benefit in the United Kingdom (widely considered a way of enriching landlords, as the payment is entirely to them, or subsidizing employers who pay poverty wages) or supply-side measures, whereby prices, including rents and purchase deposits, are capped or subsidized, as is common in parts of Austria, Denmark, Germany and the Netherlands.

Returns on investment

Investment in housing as a universal basic service will yield substantial dividends, provided that a good balance is achieved between quantity, sufficiency and affordability. Secure, sufficient housing is a route to meeting basic needs for health, autonomy and social participation across the lifetime. Conversely, homelessness or inadequate housing will act as a barrier and trigger demand for costly interventions in areas such as health care, income support and criminal justice. Where housing is designed and managed to maximize ecological sustainability, it will help to safeguard natural resources and the capacity of future generations to meet their own needs.

In summary

Everyone should have a right to housing that is secure, sufficient and affordable. That means a lot more than delivering bricks and mortar because sufficiency includes the quality of the neighbourhood and all its amenities. Residents must have control over their living conditions, and all housing must be ecologically sustainable. None of this can be delivered by markets alone. It requires collective intervention through investment, regulation and subsidy. Shortages drive up prices, so boosting or redistributing supply is vital in many areas. A UBS in housing will yield substantial social, economic and environmental gains.

Transport

There is now a growing consensus that access to motorized transport is essential for meeting basic human needs and attaining a reasonable standard of living.[9] If you cannot get from A to B, you may not be able to reach health care and other services, find and keep paid employment, meet family and friends, and generally participate in society.

There are wide variations in how far motorized transport is actually available, and to whom – whether it be public transport or privately owned vehicles. People living in rural areas often have to travel distances that are unsuitable for walking or cycling. Public transport is more likely to be patchy and unreliable outside towns and cities. People on low incomes spend a far greater proportion of their income on transport than those who are better off. They depend much more on public transport, and are affected more negatively if they cannot get access to it or find it unaffordable. So if motorized transport has become one of life's essentials, it follows that it should be available to all who need it, regardless of ability to pay.

Free bus services

Free local bus travel could be the best way to start. Buses are a ubiquitous form of public transport and free bus travel is already familiar in many countries, so there is something to build on. And buses are relatively sustainable. Free bus travel for all could help to discourage car use and reduce air pollution and GHG emissions.

Adults over 65 and disabled people can already get free bus travel in the United Kingdom. There are free local transport schemes (mainly buses) in more than a hundred towns and cities worldwide, including more than thirty in the United States and twenty in France, as well as in Poland, Sweden, Italy, Slovenia, Estonia, Australia and elsewhere. Some are restricted to certain social groups and times of day. They have been adopted for a range of reasons – to reduce social and economic inequalities, encourage social participation, discourage private-car use, cut levels of air pollution and eliminate administrative costs associated with ticketing.

A sufficient system

Rather obviously, if you don't need a ticket to ride, you still need the buses – to take you where you need to go without the kind of hassle that will put you off using them. Infrequent, poorly connected services plague much of the United Kingdom, where local buses have been deregulated (though not in London) since 1985, ostensibly to improve quality through competition. Instead, four big operators soon dominated the market, producing a patchwork of poorly connected services with no shared system of ticketing, while prices went up and government subsidies went down.[10]

Most other European countries have regulated bus services with coordinated routes and timetables, as well as better links between town and country and higher levels of public subsidy. They are more affordable and their users are more satisfied.[11]

In London, where a strategic authority has kept control of public transport, bus travel has rapidly increased, while it has declined everywhere else in the United Kingdom. Attempts to re-regulate buses outside London have failed, not least because they are locked in by powerful incumbents who lobby against reforms.[12] Falling government subsidies, meanwhile, have led to dramatic cuts in services, especially in rural areas, because local authorities are not fully compensated for the cost of providing free travel. The Local Government Association has warned that 'elderly and disabled people will be left stranded with a free bus pass in one hand but no local buses to travel on in the other'.[13]

Affordability

Analysis for the Institute for Global Prosperity found that extending free bus basses to the whole UK population would cost around £5.2 billion a year (0.26% of GDP), and the cost of extending London's level of public transport service across the United Kingdom would be £12.3 billion (0.63% GDP).[14]

The French pay for public transport through a payroll levy called *versement transport* (VT). More than 80% of France's urban transport authorities apply the levy, which pays for more than half of their infrastructure investment and subsidies to operators. Elsewhere, a huge variety of taxes are levied by local authorities around the world to pay for their public transport systems, ranging from local income and property taxes to sales and tourism taxes, corporation tax and road-user charges.[15]

Returns on investment

Spending money on buses is likely to yield a range of social, economic and environmental benefits. A 2016 evaluation of free bus travel for older and disabled people in England found that pass holders found it easier to access services, had more opportunities for social interaction and were left with more disposable income; all this disproportionately benefited poorer people.[16] Other UK studies have found that free bus travel leads to better health as a result of more physical activity (because bus travellers walk longer distances than people travelling by car), easier access to jobs, increased independence, reduced isolation, a greater sense of belonging to one's local area and contributing more to society.[17]

An analysis by KPMG of the impacts of local bus services in the United Kingdom found that 'investment in local bus markets generates significant benefits to passengers, other road users and the wider community.' Each £1 spent by government on these services produced economic, social and environmental returns ranging from £2.00 to £3.80 for revenue expenditure and from £4.20 to £8.10 for capital expenditure.[18] In a similar vein, economists at Leeds University studied the effects of improving connections between bus routes and where people wanted to go. They found that a

10% improvement in local bus service connectivity in the 10% most deprived neighbourhoods across England would lead to increased income for more than 22,000 people; nearly 10,000 more people in work; more than 7,000 more people attaining adult skills; a 0.7% increase in post-16 education; and 2,596 fewer years of life lost.[19]

Accessible, coordinated public transport across a large conurbation, even without free fares, has been estimated to reduce car traffic by 9%, resulting in better air quality and lower carbon emissions.[20] If car use were cut further by introducing free bus fares, the effect could be considerably enhanced. Greenhouse gas emissions from use of cars and taxis are more than seven times higher than from use of buses.[21] That said, a study in one German town has shown that, if you want to cut the volume of private traffic, you will get better results if you combine free public transport with strong disincentives for other road users, such as a congestion charge.[22]

In summary

Motorized transport belongs to 'a set of universal, irreducible and essential material conditions for achieving basic human well-being'.[23] It should be available to all according to need, not ability to pay. We suggest free bus travel as part of a well regulated, interconnected, frequent, reliable and adequately funded scheme that also discourages car use and encourages safe walking and cycling alongside public transport. This is not only affordable but will also yield a wide range of social, economic and environmental benefits.

Information

Digital information and communications technology (ICT) is increasingly taken for granted as one of life's essentials. Smartphones and laptops are now considered a necessary element of household expenditure and included in the agreed 'minimum income standard' for the United Kingdom.[24] The United Nations recognizes that the internet is 'a driving force in accelerating progress towards ... achieving the Sustainable Development Goals'.[25]

Going online enables people to participate in society, to learn, to find work, to connect with family and friends, and to gain access to public services. Indeed, it is likely that implementing UBS will soon depend on ICT. The UK government is aiming to put as many of its services online as possible with a 'digital by default' strategy that is 'so straightforward and convenient that all those who can use them will choose to do so'.[26] The more it becomes normal to access services online, the more difficult it will be to do so in any other way.

Unequal access

While ICT is growing exponentially, it is still a long way from being equally distributed. A 2015 report for the World Economic Forum observed that there were as many mobile subscriptions as human beings on the planet, but half of the world's population did not have mobile phones and 450 million people still lived out of reach of a mobile signal.[27] 'Digital poverty' remains widespread between and within countries. In Iceland, Norway and the Netherlands, more than 95% of households have access to the internet, but in Mexico, Costa Rica and Colombia, between a third and a half of households do not.[28]

Those most likely to lose out are rural communities (because telecommunications companies are not prepared to meet the high costs of covering greater distances, leaving signals that are poor or non-existent)[29] and poor households everywhere who can't afford the equipment or connections. There are also sharp regional inequalities in information infrastructure within countries. Many large cities in the United Kingdom can only receive broadband at speeds below the minimum standard threshold.[30]

A *utility, not a commodity*

Persistent inequalities in access to ICT have been attributed to the fact that governments have allowed market failure 'by promoting the free-market rationale and using competition as the instrument for improving digital connectivity, instead of defining new technologies as utilities'.[31] ICT should be treated not simply as a commodity for sale at market prices but as a public good or utility that is accessible, sufficient and affordable for all, as a matter of right. In other words, it should be a universal basic service.

Access depends on two main factors: a signal with sufficient capacity (speed, volume and reliability) to communicate information, and a device for using the signal to communicate. And it is worth remembering that signals and devices are a means to an end. The ultimate purpose is for people to have access to the means of participation in the social, political and economic realms.

A decade ago, internet access was primarily associated with landlines on the old telephone networks. Today it is increasingly wireless, through the mobile phone networks, which became the majority vehicle of worldwide traffic in 2016.[32] So while implementing an Information UBS is likely to involve some mix of media and technologies, depending on specific geographies, in the main it will be about providing sufficient access to wireless networks.

In most countries, the mobile networks are managed by regulated enterprises with varying degrees of competition and regulatory obligations for public interest.[33] In all cases, it has been established that the airspace through which the signals are transmitted is a public asset, and so providers bid at auctions for the rights to use certain spectra of frequencies for their transmissions, which they then lease under conditions set by the authorities, which might include maximum coverage of the population. This model served the growth of television broadcasting in the twentieth century and allows the public interest to be asserted in exchange for private use of public assets. Similar schemes enabled universal access to telephony and postal services before the television era.

It is probable that countries implementing an Information UBS will leverage these regulatory and legal structures to ensure universal access and to keep costs for the basic service to a minimum. For example, in December 2018, the UK government announced its intention to bring in legislation to ensure that universal high-speed broadband is delivered by a regulatory universal service obligation (USO), giving everyone in the United Kingdom access to speeds of at least 10 Mbps by 2020.[34]

Sufficient and affordable

What might constitute a sufficient UBS in this field? As technologies continue to develop, so will ideas about what is sufficient – and it will be a matter for informed democratic dialogue to create and review standards over time. For now, to help us get a grip on the likely costs for this UBS, let's make some assumptions and look at existing available services. A package of daily services that includes 30 minutes of talk time, 30 messages and 30MB of data can be judged to provide reasonable access to communications and to information on the World Wide Web. Commercial mobile services that include at least that amount of usage are available in many developed markets for around US$10 (up to £8) a month.[35] Public WiFi networks can provide at least that level of access at the same or lower cost. These are often created through partnerships between public, commercial and non-profit organizations. If we settle on US$120 a year per person (or a little over £90), the costs in an average OECD country[36] would be around 0.3% of GDP.

What about a device? A number of options exist here: commercial provider obligation, manufacturer contracts, and domestic production. Some combination of these means of supply could be leveraged to satisfy a diverse set of needs and provide more choice. Already commercial providers commonly include a free device with their service contracts and, even if this required additional subsidy, it would not push the cost of the service beyond reach. Given the volume of need for appropriate devices across government and service providers, it could be that the government itself would enter into a supply contract with a major manufacturer to meet its own needs and make the same available to anyone, or even go so far as to license technologies and negotiate dedicated domestic production.[37] In any case, it will cost something to make devices available, and if we allocate another US$120 (or £90-plus) per person per year to this, the total cost of the Information UBS – including communications services and devices – would be 0.6% of GDP in an average OECD country.

Digital skills

The service and the device are useless without the skills to use them. A significant part of digital exclusion is the result of a lack of skills. A 2018 survey found that 11.3 million people in the United Kingdom did not have a full set of basic digital skills, and 4.3 million had no digital skills at all. Age, gender and low income were the main predictors of low skills.[38] It is a job for education (as a universal basic service) to make digital skills more universal. This calls for reform of the primary and secondary school curricula, as well as adequate resources to ensure that schools can deliver. Adult education services will play a key role in upgrading skills in step with evolving technology.

Controlling the internet

One of the main worries people have about ICT is the growing might of a handful of global corporations and their power over governments as well as individuals. So it is important to point out here that there are now many hundreds of thousands of locally generated initiatives in towns, cities and neighbourhoods across the world whose purpose it is to keep that power at bay. They work to extend internet access by improving the speed and reach of signals, by making public spaces available (such as libraries and cafes), by sharing devices, by enabling communications within neighbourhoods through customized local platforms, by offering training in digital skills and by lobbying governments.[39]

Some work in partnership with public and/ or commercial organizations; others operate independently. Guifi-net in Barcelona describes itself as 'a bottom-up, citizenship-driven technological, social and economic project with the objective of creating a free, open and neutral telecommunications network based on a commons model'.[40] The Magnolia Road Internet Cooperative specializes in bringing high-speed internet to mountain communities in Colorado, prioritizing 'the customer over profit'.[41] 'Platform cooperatives' are a growing phenomenon, formed by nurses, delivery drivers, musicians, care providers, photographers and many others to challenge the dominance of tech giants such as Amazon and Uber by democratizing and taking back control of the internet.[42] But to call any of these typical would do no justice to their infinite variety in size, form and working practices. They are as much part of the UBS landscape in ICT as are local co-ops and other non-profit organizations in care and housing services. If they are recognized, valued and adequately supported by public authorities, they will continue to thrive and grow. They not only help to make ICT accessible and affordable, but also – crucially – they can enable people to control and shape the way they use the internet.

Potential benefits

A universal basic service is a vehicle for meeting everyday needs. It will reduce inequalities that currently arise from digital exclusion. It can help people stay in touch without having to travel. For the economy, it can help business development at all levels. A 15-year study of 35 OECD countries found a strong positive relationship between broadband investment and economic growth through information exchange, new services and telework, which together helped to increase GDP by an average of 0.38% annually.[43]

In summary

In summary, establishing a universal service in this area would require it to be recognized as a public good with access treated as a utility rather than a commodity. This UBS has a reinforcing function in that it also has the potential to make other services more efficient, flexible and deployable at scale. Governments must step in with stronger regulation and support aimed at enforcing a universal service obligation and it will be important to facilitate locally generated initiatives to make access inclusive and to support appropriate learning, especially for those who are currently excluded.

Reaching further with UBS: a note about food

As we have seen, the UBS approach is bound to take a different form in each area of need. Can we reach further, applying collective responsibility to other fields? How can we decide what is and is not included in the scope of UBS? If we start with an understanding of human need, we can identify what things are essential for people to survive and flourish. Of these, we can distinguish between, on the one hand, what people can reasonably be expected to pay for out of income based on current social norms and, on the other, where it makes sense to exercise collective responsibility to ensure that everyone has access to life's essentials and that we can meet 'the needs of the present without compromising the ability of future generations to meet their own needs'.

It is beyond the scope of this book to go into detail, but let's pause briefly to consider food as an example. Everyone needs adequate nutrition. Arguably, every society has a responsibility for ensuring that no one goes without it. It doesn't follow that governments in modern democracies have a duty to supply free food to everyone. It does follow that governments should ensure that everyone has access to the food they need and that adequate, nutritious food is available for all.

We can all agree that no child should go to school hungry, and no family should have to choose between heating and eating. We know these things happen in many rich countries, that food poverty and hunger are on the rise and that food banks – where charities provide free food – are multiplying. Food charities, such as the United Kingdom's Trussell Trust, make it clear that food banks should be an emergency response only.[44] They are not the answer to the problem of food poverty, which is linked to a complex web of factors including income insecurity and corporate profiteering, as well as poor housing, ill health, unemployment, family breakdown and social isolation.

Services that most closely match the UBS approach are those providing free meals for all schoolchildren, regardless of family income. In the United Kingdom, free school meals are provided to all pupils in reception and years one and two, but thereafter the service is means tested. Three London councils provide free school lunches to all primary school pupils, while a fourth, Hammersmith and Ealing, provides free breakfasts for all primary school pupils, regardless of family income, and is piloting delivery of free lunches to all pupils in two secondary schools from 2020. The aim is to make good the failings of the means-tested system, which has been found to stigmatize and exclude too many, and to improve children's well-being and educational performance overall.[45] Finland has provided universal free school meals since 1943, and children can now get free hot lunches in Helsinki's parks during the summer months.[46]

Alongside free school meals, a radically improved social security system would make a huge contribution to enabling people to meet their food needs. So would high-quality public services that meet needs for education, health and care, housing, transport and information – because each of these, in different ways, contributes to, or removes barriers from healthy eating. But these are not the whole answer to the question of how to ensure that everyone gets the food they need.

It also matters what kind of food people can obtain and afford, and whether it is sufficiently nutritious to enable them to flourish. What shapes our eating habits? Are fresh fruit and vegetables available and affordable? Why do so many people have diets that are heavy in salt, sugar and saturated fats? How far do patterns of food consumption affect – and depend on – the natural environment? How do my food preferences affect the livelihoods and diets of other people?

Applying UBS to food would require a whole-systems approach. We might start with the proposition that everyone has a right to sufficient, nutritious food. Realizing that right would involve policies for trade and agriculture that support sustainable food production, regulation of business to promote healthy, affordable food, and statutory controls of advertising and sales to restrict foodstuffs that are harmful. There would be policies to enable as much food as possible to be grown, sold and consumed locally, to reduce 'food miles' with high emissions, to support local initiatives that promote collective food production and consumption, and to make sure good food is available everywhere so that there are no more 'food deserts' in disadvantaged neighbourhoods. Health and education services would encourage healthy eating and work together to build knowledge across the population about what's good to eat and why it matters. Schools, hospitals, childcare centres, care homes and other public institutions would supply appetizing, nutritious meals for all who use their services. A radically reformed social security system would ensure that everyone can afford to buy enough food. Food banks would be history.

So a food UBS would not mean providing a single service but developing a comprehensive set of policies and practices. It would amount to a constellation of collectively generated activities that serve the public interest by shaping and coordinating production, distribution and consumption of food, so that healthy eating becomes the norm and everyone has access to affordable, nutritious, sustainable food. The fact that this is a complicated proposition is not, in our view, a reason for leaving food off the UBS agenda. It does show that, when it comes to meeting some needs, private purchase and collective responsibility are two sides of the same coin.

6

Challenges and Responses

Because the proposal for UBS is new, it has not yet attracted much in the way of direct challenge. Various critiques have begun to emerge, and they can roughly be summarized as follows. UBS would lead to big government, centralized power, paternalism and social engineering. The state is not competent to realize the vision. There is lack of clarity about how decisions would be made. It could lead to further accumulation by big business. It would run into strong resistance from those with an interest in the status quo. It is incompatible with capitalism and requires radical transformation, not piecemeal reform.[1] Last but not least, there are bound to be questions about how much it costs and whether it is affordable.

These are valid points. There is clearly a great

deal more work to be done to flesh out aspirations for UBS, its philosophical bases, costs and benefits, and the nuts and bolts of implementation. We have only embarked on the first stage of the journey, but we can begin to address some of the challenges, based on our work so far.

Power and competence of government

The extent to which any UBS system would enhance the power of central government will depend partly on how far power is devolved to localities. But localism is not in itself a recipe for better policy or practice. That depends on the structures and political strategies that operate locally and nationally.[2]

We have made it clear that services should be provided by a range of organizations with diverse models of ownership, rather than always being directly provided by government. With more devolution and a reformed tax system, we can envisage more localized power to raise money for investment in services. However, it will be crucial for central government to retain key functions – not least to ensure that everyone has access to sufficient services, wherever they live, on the basis of need, not ability to pay. This points to a system of central government investment to supplement local funds, adjusted for equitable distribution between localities.

As for the competence of government to implement UBS, we have no illusions about grafting this proposal onto the status quo. Integral to the idea, as we hope we have made clear, is a new kind of relationship between local, regional and national governments, and significant changes in the culture and practice of public authorities. We want to see those authorities transformed so that they generate and support different ways of delivering services and enabling people to meet their needs. There are lessons to be learned from cities such as Barcelona in Spain, Bologna in Italy, Ghent in Belgium, Cleveland in Ohio, USA and Preston in Lancashire, UK, where authorities have committed themselves in various ways to enabling local people to gain more control over access to life's necessities.

In Barcelona, for example, Barcelona en Comú, described as a 'citizen platform', has led the city government in promoting what it calls a collaborative economy, including many hundreds of cooperatives and other community-led and public interest organizations. In Bologna, the city government has introduced a pioneering regulation for 'the care and regeneration of urban commons' and has entered into more than 90 different 'pacts of collaboration' with citizen groups, including collaborative services, shared enterprises and co-production. The Flemish city of Ghent has endorsed an ambitious 'commons transition plan', which promotes a model of 'poly-governance', with state, markets and civil society working together to support and scale up locally generated social and economic initiatives. In Cleveland, Ohio, the Evergreen Cooperative Initiative works with local businesses, foundations and public sector organizations to transform poor neighbourhoods by creating living wage jobs in local cooperatives.[3] Inspired by this approach, council leaders in Preston, UK, began to lift the city out of apparently irreversible decline by encouraging new cooperative ventures and credit unions, and persuading public bodies operating in the area to spend their money locally.

All these ventures have encountered criticism, even from local progressive organizations, and it would be foolish to idealize them. This is work in progress. What they all show is a willingness to transform relationships between local government and local residents, shifting power outwards to a wide variety of groups and organizations, many of which could – or already do – play a part in designing and delivering services under local control.

Decision making

A democratic framework for making decisions would be essential. The New Economics Foundation (among others) has proposed 'a dialogue that combines lay people along with professionals (in service delivery, for example) and other experts, and with democratically elected representatives'.[4] This approach could be used at local, regional or national level to determine what needs should be met collectively and to design services and other appropriate activities. It combines elements of par ticipatory and representative democracy, and builds on experience of citizens' juries, deliberative polling, people's forums, town-hall meetings and similar initiatives in the United States, Europe and elsewhere.

Among notable examples is Ireland's citizens' assembly convened between 2016 and 2018 to consider a range of questions including the law on abortion.[5] Lay members were selected to represent a broad cross-section of the population. They considered evidence and discussed relevant questions with experts, as well as among themselves, and drew conclusions through consensus. Their conclusions led to a referendum that legalized abortion. This kind of framework for three-way deliberative dialogue is not intended to replace representative democracy but to revive and enrich it by drawing closer to the views, values and everyday experiences of the people it is supposed to represent.

Profiteering by big corporations

There is a risk of UBS maximizing profits for big corporations if they are allowed to dominate an expanding market in service provision. This can be avoided if UBS is embedded – as we envisage – in a well-regulated system with multiple providers and measures to encourage and support public bodies and other non-profit organizations. It would mean bringing for-profit and non-profit organizations within a shared framework of values, goals and expectations, at the same time strengthening the role of non-profits in the economy. The EU's Commission for Sustainable Equality recommends new measures to build and support the 'social and solidarity economy', so that it ceases to be merely an 'add-on' or limited alternative to the dominant profit-seeking model but instead becomes a 'long-term mainstream model for a truly sustainable economy', in social, environmental and democratic terms.[6]

Challenges and Responses

The Manchester School proposes a system of *social licensing* that would make the right to trade dependent on 'providing a service, plus meeting negotiated criteria of community responsibility on issues such as sourcing, training and payment of living wages'.[7] This follows current practice in many European countries and could lend force and definition to the otherwise woolly concept of 'corporate social responsibility'.

Meeting resistance

How to meet the challenge of winning and sustaining electoral support for UBS? Establishing a framework for democratic dialogue could certainly help, judging by Ireland's recent experience of a citizens' assembly, or Scotland's 1995 Constitutional Convention, which prepared the ground for devolution and the first Scottish Parliament in 1999.[8] Changes should be introduced gradually to iron out mistakes, demonstrate successes where possible and give people opportunities to learn from experience.

If the process of change is incremental, service contracts can be altered as they come up for renewal to improve access and quality and to strengthen public participation. Incumbent providers are bound to resist such changes. The larger and richer they are, the heavier their influence is likely to be. How far they prevail will depend on the political and economic environment in which changes are introduced.

The question of whether UBS is incompatible with capitalism is worth asking. Capitalism is not intrinsically antithetical to exercising collective responsibility to meet shared needs, as the post-war settlements have shown. The current neoliberal phase of capitalism prefers a small state and a free market, which are not conditions in which UBS can flourish. But there are still varieties both of capitalism and of welfare regimes in different countries across the world – some less hostile and more conducive to UBS than prevailing models in the Anglosphere. Can some of these coexist comfortably with universal basic services? We hope there will be more debate on the question. But we probably won't find out until we test the idea in practice.

How much would it cost and is it affordable?

This is an ambitious proposal, and it is reasonable to ask whether services we wish to make universally affordable for individuals can also be collectively affordable.

Costings for all proposed new services, plus the improvements that should be made to existing universal services, will vary between services and between countries. We do not attempt to calculate them in specific detail. In each proposed new area set out in chapters 4 and 5, we have provided some indicative costs using sample data from a range of sources. To make these relatively consistent across countries, we have used a percentage of GDP (gross domestic product) as the common metric. Of course, most OECD countries already spend significant amounts on health, care, transport and access to digital information, and some services in some countries already offer universal access. In no country is a full range of our proposed services provided universally. We estimate that the total additional annual expenditure required for the services we propose, if implemented all at once, would be around 4.3% of GDP in a typical OECD country. Below is a brief summary of how we have arrived at our figures (summarized in Figure 6.1).

- *Child care.* As an indicator of the budget required to provide decent child care as a universal service we use the figure of 1.4% of GDP, derived from

	% GDP
Transport	0.4%
Information & Communications	0.6%
Child care	1.4%
Adult social care	1.4%
Housing	0.5%
	4.3%

Figure 6.1 Proposed spending on UBS as percentage of GDP

an average of the four most generous countries' current spending on child care (p. 64).

- *Adult social care.* We have used projections of the extra costs over and above healthcare spending, while acknowledging large differences in the balance between formal provision and informal care in different countries. The OECD 30 average for 2014 was 1.4% of GDP and we have used this to indicate a starting point for expenditure (p. 70).

- *Housing.* Based on a significant expansion of social-rent housing, we have budgeted 0.5% GDP using estimates from the IGP UBS report (2017). In this case, capital costs are spread over a 30-year bond issue, and savings from unneeded future housing benefits are taken into account. Enormous differences between countries in land

and building costs, as well as existing stock of socially rented properties, make this a hard service to budget uniformly across countries, but a commitment of 0.5% of GDP would certainly have a significant impact in any country (p. 84).

- *Transport*. A budget of 0.4% of GDP for enhanced transport represents a reasonable estimate for additional spending required to provide universal access to local transport to reach employment and other public services (p. 90).[9]
- *Information*. Around 0.6% of GDP could cover both service access and devices in a typical OECD country, although alternatives such as public WiFi could significantly reduce the per-person costs in some areas (p. 98).

An expansive UBS programme along the lines we suggest would represent a significant increase in current public spending. To put this in perspective, however, our figure represents less than 15% of total government spending in every OECD country except Chile and Ireland.[10] In the late 1940s, UK government spending rose by some 20% of GDP to fund post-war reconstruction and the new welfare state. More recently, in 2008, both UK and USA governments increased public spending by more than 6% of GDP to cope with the financial crisis.[11]

While these events are not directly comparable, they do suggest that, when governments decide to increase spending, it is more a matter of political choice than applying rules of contemporary economics.

It is worth noting that our costings do not account for the potential savings that can be generated by a radical shift towards UBS. First, there are likely to be economies of scale where needs are met collectively rather than individually. Second, we want services to be organized to enable people to co-produce – as far as possible – the ways in which their needs are met. By bringing uncommodified human resources into the process, this can not only improve the well-being of the individuals concerned – provided they are adequately supported – but also improve the quality and scope of the services without a corresponding increase in the overall cost. We believe this can be done by transforming the policies and practices of public institutions, rather than by 'dumping' state responsibilities on poor communities. Third, collective action to meet needs can prevent harm that would otherwise require more costly interventions. Fourth, UBS can generate considerable returns on investment in social and ecological as well as economic terms.

Where would the money come from? The main

options for generating public funds for UBS are: raising existing taxes, creating new taxes, borrowing, and redistributing funds from other areas of government spending. We have noted that borrowing (by issuing long-term government bonds) is a suitable option for investing in some aspects of the material infrastructure, such as housing. But to keep things simple here, we will concentrate on taxation and revenue options available across countries with both shared and sovereign currencies. Figure 6.2 reveals the wide discrepancy in total tax takes across the OECD.

The OECD average is 34% of GDP, but many EU member states exceed this proportion and in France, Denmark, Sweden and Italy it is well over 40% of GDP. Tax revenues in the 'anglophone' countries are below average: in the United Kingdom 33%, Canada 32%, Australia 28% and the United States 27%. Tax regimes and other revenue-raising policies also vary widely between countries. They depend on political support and this, in turn, depends on specific national factors including history and culture. In some countries, local governments have far stronger revenue-raising powers; in federal systems, such as the United States and Germany, states have considerable fiscal autonomy. Given this variation in the size and composition of taxes, it is simply not

119

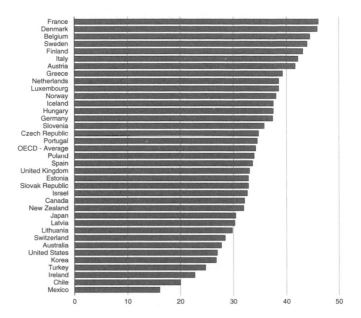

Figure 6.2 Tax revenues in OECD countries as % of GDP

Source: OECD[12]

possible to make general recommendations here as to what should be raised to cover the cost of UBS. Thus we concentrate on the United Kingdom.

For the United Kingdom and similar low-tax countries, there is considerable fiscal space for a UBS costing an additional 4% of GDP. Figure 6.3 shows that this would take UK tax levels up to – but not beyond – the levels prior to the sharp drop around 1980. As we note in our concluding chapter, there appears to be support for increased spending on public services.

Whatever means are chosen for raising funds to pay for UBS, there are three caveats. First, tax reforms should be designed to safeguard the value of disposable income for low-income families. While income taxes are usually arranged progressively, with rates rising as one climbs the income scale, consumption taxes such as VAT are regressive because lower-income households spend a higher portion of their incomes on basic necessities. One suggestion (in our view worth pursuing but beyond the scope of this book) is to make consumption taxes more progressive via a 'smart VAT' levied at higher rates on luxury and unsustainable consumer goods.[13]

The second caveat is that revenue-raising systems should reinforce rather than undermine solidarity. UBS aims to ensure that everyone has equal access to services that meet their needs, regardless of where they live or how much money they have. In areas where incomes are low, needs are often greater. If services rely on locally generated resources, then poor neighbourhoods are bound to find themselves with poor services. This calls for a strong role for national/federal governments to raise and distribute funds equitably and to supplement locally generated resources.

At the same time, it will be important for revenues to be raised across the broadest population: the greater the numbers who make a contribution, the stronger the base for collective responsibility. In recent years, many governments have sought to remove those on the lowest incomes from liability for income taxes. While this may seem both equitable and politically expedient, it has two negative effects: it increases pressure to raise sales taxes, which are regressive, and it drives democratic power away from the bottom of the income scale towards those already at the top. Ultimately, it can damage the democratic fabric of society and the common acceptance of taxation as part of the social contract.

The third caveat is to respect the need for public funds required for other things that are important for a progressive policy agenda. One example is making the transition to a sustainable economy, which means developing renewable energy, retrofitting homes, transforming transport systems and much more. Another is reforming social security (or social protection) so that everyone has access to a living income as well as a social wage.

With these caveats in mind, let's look briefly at

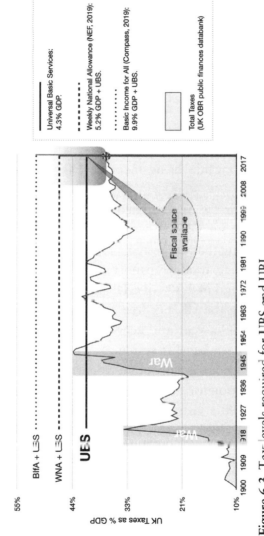

Figure 6.3 Tax levels required for UBS and UBI

the option of reducing personal tax-free allowances (a form of hidden or 'shadow' public spending as it is money forgone by the Treasury). As they stand, these allowances benefit better-off taxpayers, making them a popular target with progressive reformers. Three recent UK policy proposals adopt this approach. We mention them here because they shed light on issues that arise when considering UBS alongside basic income schemes (see Figure 6.3).

The first is the original UBS proposal from the Institute for Global Prosperity. This was based on modelling that suggested a range of services, including shelter, food, transport and information, which cost a total of 2.3% of GDP and could be funded by reducing the UK tax-free allowance from £11,000 to £4,300 a year and keeping the existing compensatory cash benefits system.

The second is a proposal from the New Economics Foundation for a weekly national allowance (WNA) of £2,500 a year for all adults, with an increase in existing child benefits and all means-tested benefits retained. This would be funded by redistributing the whole of the value of the tax-free allowance at a cost of 5.2% of GDP a year. The authors insist that the WNA is not a partial UBI or even a route to one, and it is designed to be compatible with a programme of radically expanded public services and social infrastructure.

The third example comes from Compass, the London-based campaign group. They propose a partial UBI ranging from £3,120 per annum for working-age adults, £2,080 for children and £9,100 for people over 65. All existing means-tested benefits would be retained, and they introduce a new lower rate of income tax for low earners to keep the overall effect progressive. It would be paid for partly by replacing various non-means-tested benefits and pensions, and partly by abolishing the entire tax-free allowance. That still leaves a shortfall of £61 billion, which they propose to cover by raising income tax rates and national insurance contributions. This would have progressive effects, but it would still be a long way short of sufficient to live on and would cost 9.9% of GDP – more than twice as much as our proposal for a UBS.

UBS should certainly be accompanied by a programme to reform social security benefits with the aims of reducing complexity and means testing. A universal minimum income (or weekly national allowance) could be considered as part of this reform, but even a modest basic income scheme would be far less compatible with UBS. Quite apart from the ideological gulf we have described, it would swallow up available funds – and more – that could be earmarked for other progressive objectives, from housing to social infrastructure to green investment and eco-maintenance. We can't spend the same money twice. If we must rob Peter to pay Paul, we should be sure we are making a worthwhile exchange.

So is UBS affordable? Certainly. A UBS programme costing 4% of GDP is within reach of every OECD country without exceeding commonly accepted bounds of fiscal propriety, and for lower-income countries it is likely that the package of services would be tailored to suit their development path. It is one of the great strengths of the UBS proposal that it builds on what already exists and can be introduced incrementally without sudden shocks to the system.

Conclusions

UBS is not a religion requiring conversion. It is a call for radical change in direction that will be shaped by experience. We don't expect any country to switch on a full array of UBS overnight. There will be both temporal and fiscal space in which to experiment with incremental change to enhance existing services and develop new ones.

Although UBS is an incremental programme, it presents a radical challenge to today's dominant political and economic paradigm, as we have shown. The greatest obstacle comes from defenders of current norms, who tell us that change is undesirable or impossible, or both. So it is worth taking a moment to consider the phenomenon of rapid transition. This is where changes that were once inconceivable to all but a marginal few become

127

possible, then normal within a matter of decades, until finally it is inconceivable to return to the status quo ante. The end of the transatlantic slave trade, votes for women and the ban on smoking in public places are all examples. In each case, transition is propelled by similar factors: mounting evidence in support of change, growing movements that campaign for change, leaders capable of harnessing momentum and articulating how change can happen and (often if not always) a crisis to upset the applecart of convention.

We hope we have demonstrated that there is mounting evidence in favour of a change in direction towards UBS. There is also a chain of linked crises in the social, economic and environmental conditions that confront populations worldwide. We are still waiting for the right kind of leadership, but this is likely to grow out of a movement for change.

Is there such a movement? Recent shifts in public attitudes and a flowering of like-minded political initiatives suggest there is one taking shape. The idea of 'austerity' as a route to economic success has run its course and is now widely rejected by economists,[1] as well as by the public. As the *Financial Times* reported in September 2018, 'British people are fed up with austerity'; two-thirds now say they are willing to pay more tax in return for more spending on health and education, representing 'the highest level of support for public services since 2002'.[2]

An OECD survey of public attitudes to risk in 21 countries found that almost half of Americans said they would pay an additional 2% income tax to receive better health care, and one-third would be prepared to pay a 2% levy in return for better state education. This was consistent with the pattern across all countries in the survey. In general, people are more worried than they used to be about risks to their well-being and livelihoods, about security in old age and their children's prospects; they are distrustful of governments and dissatisfied with current arrangements for social protection; they want more collective provision and many are prepared to pay for it. Between 50% and 80% in all countries agree or strongly agree that the government should 'tax the rich more than they currently do in order to support the poor'.[3] Similarly, the European Social Survey found in 2018 that there was strong support among Europeans for welfare redistribution and for national governments having 'responsibility for the wellbeing of vulnerable groups'.[4]

These attitudes don't constitute a movement, but they help to create conditions in which a movement can grow and thrive. We shouldn't expect a single trajectory, with everything moving in the same direction at the same time. But we can detect promising signs in a range of political developments, from the temporary flourishing of protest parties such as Podemos in Spain and the global Occupy movement, to the enduring Transition Towns network, Extinction Rebellion and the climate protests of schoolchildren in 2019. As experts in radical transition insist, 'our collective capacity, ability and resourcefulness for change is much higher than is typically recognised'.[5]

While working on this book, we have been inspired by many others who are thinking along the same lines. This has strengthened our conviction that there is a burgeoning enthusiasm for the principles of UBS: exercising collective responsibility to meet shared needs. Out of a rich field, we will mention just three, which feature in our earlier chapters. The first is the Manchester School's work on the Foundational Economy, published in 2018, proposing a 'systems based redistribution which expands universal entitlement to services'.[6] They focus on everyday necessities and the connections between local and national politics; they offer a clear view of what truly constitutes an 'economy', its moral underpinnings and practical implications.

Conclusions

The second is the Independent Commission for Sustainable Equality, convened by the Progressive Alliance of Socialists and Democrats in the European Parliament. This maps out a just transition to sustainable development by empowering people and reshaping capitalism. Its 2018 report is imbued with a sense of urgency and proposes (among much else) a Common Wealth Charter to 'ensure that every person would have a guarantee of free-of-charge access to a set of essential services, such as education, medical treatment, public transport, or culture, and an access at low cost to a set of essential goods, including food and water, energy, land and housing'.

The third is the proposal by Alexandria Ocasio-Cortez in the US Congress in 2019 that the federal government should recognize its duty to create a Green New Deal. This ambitious, wide-ranging proposal reinvents the Roosevelt New Deal in modern terms, calling for an inclusive, participative and socially just programme for environmental sustainability. Along with net-zero greenhouse gas emissions, the creation of millions of good high-wage jobs and investment in infrastructure to meet the challenges of the twenty-first century, the Green New Deal seeks to provide 'all people of the United States' with high-quality health care; affordable, safe and adequate housing; economic security; and clean water, clean air, healthy and affordable food, and access to nature.[7]

Of course, none of these initiatives will trigger immediate action, but that's not the point. They are straws in the wind. They emerge from and contribute to a tidal shift in 'common sense' about what is desirable and possible. Our proposal is part of that shift and we hope it makes a further contribution.

So, to conclude, here are ten points to sum up our argument.

1　'UBS' describes services or other activities that are essential and sufficient to enable people to meet their needs and flourish, available to all, regardless of ability to pay.

2　It rests on two principles: collective responsibility and shared needs – exercising the first to meet the second.

3　The UBS agenda includes health care, education and other existing universal services, and extends into new areas such as child care, adult social care, housing, transport and information.

4　UBS requires a customized approach to each area of need, and there is much to be learned from existing services, as well as from other countries.

5　It is not about uniformity or top-down delivery, but a wide variety of collective activities, conducted through many different organizations under local control, to which people have equal rights of access.

6　It calls for a new dynamic between top-down and bottom-up politics, with power devolved as far as possible and the national state retaining four key functions: to ensure equality of access; to set and enforce standards; to collect and invest funds; and to coordinate functions across sectors to maximize social, environmental and economic outcomes.

7　UBS promises to bring substantial benefits across four dimensions: equality; efficiency; solidarity; and sustainability.

8　It should be accompanied by a more generous, less conditional and non-stigmatizing system of social security that gives everyone the right to a living income.

9　An extended programme of UBS can be both sufficient and affordable but cannot be implemented alongside a sufficient universal cash payment (or basic income) scheme, due to conflict of purpose and competition for funds.

10　There is a growing movement for radical change in opposition to today's dominant political consensus that rests on neoliberal economics, social injustice and climate change denial. The case for UBS belongs to that movement.

Notes

Introduction

1 A formal definition of a 'service', as distinct from a 'good', is a type of activity that is intangible, is not stored, does not result in ownership and is used at the point of delivery.
2 Social Prosperity Network (2017), 'Social Prosperity for the Future: A Proposal for Universal Basic Services', UCL: IGP.
3 A. Coote and E. Yazici (2019), 'Universal Basic Income: A Briefing for Trade Unions', Ferney-Voltaire, France: Public Services International.

Chapter 1 Why We Need This Change

1 P. Alston (2017), 'Statement on Visit to the USA', Geneva: United Nations.

2 P. Alston (2018), 'Statement on Visit to the United Kingdom', Geneva: United Nations.
3 M. Nussbaum (2000), *Women and Human Development: The Capabilities Approach*, Cambridge: Cambridge University Press.
4 L. Doyal and I. Gough (1991), *A Theory of Human Need*, London: Palgrave Macmillan, p. 4.
5 Ibid., fig. 1, p. 25; S. C. Miller (2012), *The Ethics of Need: Agency, Dignity and Obligation*, New York: Routledge.
6 N. D. Rao and J. Min (2017), 'Decent Living Standards: Material Requisites for Human Well Being', *Journal of Social Indicators Research* 138(1): 138–225.
7 E. Durkheim (1984), *The Division of Labour in Society*, London: Palgrave Macmillan, pp. 154–9.
8 T. Marshall (1965), 'The Right to Welfare', *The Sociological Review* 13(3): 261–72.
9 A. Sayer (2000), 'Moral Economy and Political Economy', *Studies in Political Economy* 61(1): 79–103.
10 R. Tawney (1964), *Equality*, 5th edn, London: Allen and Unwin.
11 Brundtland Commission (1987), *Our Common Future*, Oxford: Oxford University Press.

Chapter 2 How Would It Work in Practice?

1 H. Evans and D. Wellings (2017), 'What Does the Public Think about the NHS?'. https://www.kingsfund.org.uk/publications/what-does-public-think-about-nhs.

2 C. Saunders (2017), 'Attitudes to Education and Children's Services: The British Social Attitudes Survey 2016', London: Department for Education.
3 J. Froud et al. (2018), *Foundational Economy*, Manchester: Manchester University Press, p. 40.
4 We use the term 'service user' as shorthand for people who use services, and to distinguish them from residents or citizens, who may not currently be using services but may need them at other times.
5 A. Coote (2010), 'Ten Big Questions about the Big Society', London: NEF; L. Findlay-King, Geoff Nichols, Deborah Forbes and Gordon Macfadyen (2018), 'Localism and the Big Society: The Asset Transfer of Leisure Centres and Libraries – Fighting Closures or Empowering Communities?', *Leisure Studies* 37(2): 158–70.
6 E. Turner (2019), 'Empowering Local Government or Just Passing the Austerity Buck? The Changing Balance of Central and Local Government in Welfare Provision in England 2008–2015', *Regional & Federal Studies* 29(1): 45–65.
7 J. McCarthy (2005), 'Commons as Counter-hegemonic Projects', *Capitalism Nature Socialism* 16(1): 9–24, 17.
8 J. Angel (2014), 'Moving Beyond the Market: A New Agenda for Public Services', London: NEF, pp. 35–41; A. Cumbers (2012), *Reclaiming Public Ownership*, London: Zed Books; H. Wainwright (2009), *Reclaim the State: Experiments in Popular Democracy*, London: Seagull Books.

9 Independent Commission on Sustainable Equality (2018), 'Wellbeing for Everyone in a Sustainable Europe', Progressive Alliance of Socialists and Democrats in the European Parliament, pp. 17, 75.

10 Froud and Williams, *Foundational Economy*, pp. 108–10.

11 N. Goodwin (2018), 'There is More Than One Economy', *The Real-World Economics Review* 84: 16–35, 24; M. Hill (2014), 'It's the Economic Value, Stupid, but is Volunteering Really Worth £100bn to the UK?'. https://blogs.ncvo.org.uk/2014/06/26/its-the-economic-value-stupidbut-is-volunteering-really-worth-100bn-to-the-uk/.

12 J. Konings (2010), 'Childcare Vouchers: Who Benefits?', London: Social Market Foundation, p. 7; C. Wood and J. Salter (2013), *The Power of Prepaid*, London: Demos, pp. 9–15.

13 A. Coote (2017), 'Building a New Social Commons: The People, the Commons and the Public Realm', London: NEF, p. 5; L. Stephens (2008), 'Co-Production: A Manifesto for Growing the Core Economy', London: NEF, pp. 9–12.

14 D. Boyle, A. Coote, C. Sherwood and J. Slay (2010), 'Right Here, Right Now: Taking Co-production into the Mainstream', London: Nesta, p. 13.

15 P. Beresford (2019), 'Austerity is Denying Patients and Care Service Users a Voice', *The Guardian*. https://www.theguardian.com/society/2019/jan/14/austerity-denying-patients-care-service-users-voice.

16 Atkinson was considering eligibility for income support but the concept can equally apply to services.

17 A. B. Atkinson (2015), *Inequality: What Can Be Done?*, Cambridge, MA: Harvard University Press, p. 219.
18 A. Coote (2017), 'Building a New Social Commons', London: NEF, p. 16.
19 Finlex Databank (n.d.), 'Social Rights'. http://www. finlex.fi/fi/laki/kaannokset/1999/en19990731.pdf; http://www.kela.fi/web/en/social-rights.
20 The Belgian Constitution, Article 23. http://www. const-court.be/en/basic_text/belgian_constitution.pdf.
21 C. Reich (1965), 'Individual Rights and Social Welfare: The Emerging Legal Issues', *Yale Law Journal* 74(7): 1252–3; D. Galligan (1992), 'Procedural Rights in Social Welfare', in A. Coote (ed.), *The Welfare of Citizens: Developing New Social Rights*, London: IPPR/Rivers Oram Press, pp. 55–68; R. Hirschl (2013), 'The Strategic Foundations of Constitutions', in D. Galligan and M. Veerstag (eds), *Social and Political Foundations of Constitutions*, Cambridge: Cambridge University Press, p. 162.

Chapter 3 The Benefits of UBS

1 G. Verbist, M. Förster and M. Vaalavuo (2012), 'The Impact of Publicly Provided Services on the Distribution of Resources: Review of New Results and Methods', OECD Social, Employment and Migration Working Papers 130: 35.
2 Ibid., pp. 25–6.
3 R. G. Wilkinson and K. Pickett (2010), *The Spirit Level: Why Greater Equality Makes Societies Stronger*, New York: Bloomsbury Press.

4 M. Evandrou, J. Falkingham, J. Hills and J. Le Grand (1993), 'Welfare Benefits in Kind and Income Distribution', *Fiscal Studies* 14(1): 57–76.

5 T. Sefton (2002), 'Recent Changes in the Distribution of the Social Wage', CASE Paper 62, London: LSE, p. 46; ONS (2018), 'Effects of Taxes and Benefits on UK Household Income: Financial Year Ending 2017', Section 4, Fig. 5.

6 I. Gough (2008), 'European Welfare States: Explanations and Lessons for Developing Countries', in A. Dani and A. D. Haan (eds), *Inclusive States: Social Policy and Structural Inequalities*, Washington, DC: World Bank, p. 42.

7 A. Wahl (2011), *The Rise and Fall of the Welfare State*, London: Pluto Press, pp. 122–3.

8 M. Raco (2013), 'The New Contractualism, the Privatization of the Welfare State, and the Barriers to Open Source Planning', *Planning Practice & Research* 28(1): 45–64.

9 LGA (2012), 'Services Shared: Costs Spared?'. https://www.local.gov.uk/sites/default/files/documents/services-shared-costs-spa-61b.pdf; OECD (2015), *Building on Basics, Value for Money in Government*, Paris: OECD Publishing, pp. 145–63.

10 S. Brownlee (2007), *Overtreated: Why Too Much Medicine is Making Us Sicker and Poorer*, New York: Bloomsbury, pp. 99–109; 206; N. Modi et al. (2018), 'Health Systems Should Be Publicly Funded and Publicly Provided', *British Medical Journal* 362(k3580).

11 ONS (2016), 'How Does UK Healthcare Spending

Compare Internationally?'. https://www.ons.gov.
uk/peoplepopulationandcommunity/healthandsocial
care/healthcaresystem/articles/howdoesukhealthcare
spendingcompareinternationally/2016-11-01.

12 A. Gulland (2011), 'UK Healthcare System is One
of Most Efficient in Rich Countries', *British Medical
Journal* 343(d5143).

13 DCMS (2018), 'The Public Services (Social Value)
Act 2012: Introductory Guide', p. 2.

14 M. Bauwens and V. Niaros (2017), 'Value in the
Commons Economy: Developments in Open and
Contributory Value Accounting', Heinrich Böll
Foundation and P2P Foundation, p. 3.

15 A. Coote and J. Angel (2014), 'Solidarity: Why it
Matters for a New Social Settlement', London: NEF
Working Paper.

16 E. Durkheim (1984 [1893]), *The Division of Labour
in Society*, London: Palgrave Macmillan, pp. 154–9.

17 European Commission (1997), 'First Report on
Economic and Social Cohesion 1996', Luxembourg:
Office for Official Publications of the European
Commission.

18 J. Kääriäinen and H. Lehtonen (2006), 'The
Variety of Social Capital in Welfare State Regimes
– A Comparative Study of 21 Countries', *European
Sociation* 8(1), 27–57, W. V. Oorschot and W. Arts
(2005), 'The Social Capital of European Welfare States:
The Crowding Out Hypothesis Revisited', *Journal
of European Social Policy* 15(1): 5–26; B. Rothstein
and D. Stolle (2003), 'Social Capital in Scandinavia',
Scandinavian Political Studies 26(1): 1–25.

19 M. Sandel (2012), 'How Markets Crowd Out Morals', *The Boston Review* (May).

20 R. Titmuss et al. (1997), *The Gift Relationship*, New York: The New Press.

21 M. Sandel (2013), *What Money Can't Buy: The Moral Limits of Markets*, London: Penguin, pp. 64–5; J. Dean (2015), 'Volunteering, the Market, and Neoliberalism', *People, Place and Policy* 9(2): 139–48.

22 K. Lynch and M. Kalaitzake (2018), 'Affective and Calculative Solidarity: The Impact of Individualism and Neoliberal Capitalism', *European Journal of Social Theory*: 1–20; J. M. Brodie (2007), 'Reforming Social Justice in Neoliberal Times', *Studies in Social Science* 1(2); K. Jayasuriya (2006), *Statecraft, Welfare and the Politics of Inclusion*, Basingstoke: Palgrave Macmillan, p. 15.

23 P. Ekins (2014), 'Strong Sustainability and Critical Natural Capital', in G. Atkinson, S. Dietz, E. Neumayer and M. Agarwala (eds), *Handbook of Sustainable Development*, Cheltenham: Edward Elgar Publishing, p. 56.

24 A. Coote (2015), 'People, Planet Power: Towards a New Social Settlement', London: NEF, p. 19.

25 R. Freeman (1992), 'The Idea of Prevention: A Critical Review', in S. J. Scott, G. Williams, S. Platt and H. Thomas (eds), *Private Risks and Public Dangers*, Aldershot: Avebury; I. Gough (2015), 'The Political Economy of Prevention', *British Journal of Political Science* 45(2): 307–27.

26 Independent Commission on Sustainable Equality,

'Wellbeing for Everyone in a Sustainable Europe', pp. 74–5.

27 I. Gough (2017), *Heat, Greed and Human Need*, Cheltenham: Edward Elgar, p. 163.

28 I. Gough et al. (2008), 'Climate Change and Social Policy: A Symposium', *Journal of European Social Policy* 18(4): 325–44.

29 Green New Deal Group (2008), 'A Green New Deal', London: NEF, p. 3.

30 I. Ortiz et al. (2018), 'Universal Basic Income Proposals in Light of ILO Standards: Key Issues and Global Costing', Geneva: ILO, p. 13.

31 Ibid., p. 29.

32 The *Guardian* Letters (2016), 'Potential Benefits and Pitfalls of a UBI', *The Guardian*. https://www.the guardian.com/politics/2016/jun/10/potential-benef its-and-pitfalls-of-a-universal-basic-income.

33 F. Mestrum (2018), 'Why Basic Income Can Never Be a Progressive Solution', in A. Downes and S. Lansley (eds), *It's Basic Income: The Global Debate*, Bristol: Policy Press, pp. 97–8.

34 F. Whitfield (2018), 'Why Basic Income is Not Good Enough', in A. Downes and S. Lansley (eds), *It's Basic Income: The Global Debate*, Bristol: Policy Press, pp. 109–12.

Chapter 4 Rolling Out UBS: Meeting Needs for Care

1 We use the term 'child care' throughout this section to denote early childhood care and education for pre-school children.

2 E. Lloyd and S. Potter (2014), 'Early Childhood Education and Care and Poverty', working paper for Joseph Rowntree Foundation, London: University of East London, p. 78.

3 H. May (2014), 'New Zealand: A Narrative of Shifting Policy Directions for Early Childhood Education and Care', in L. Gambaro, K. Stewart and J. Waldfogel, *An Equal Start? Providing Quality Early Childhood Education and Care for Disadvantaged Children*, Bristol: Policy Press, pp. 147–8.

4 K. Stewart et al. (2014), 'Common Challenges, Lessons for Policy', in L. Gambaro, K. Stewart and J. Waldfogel, *An Equal Start? Providing Quality Early Childhood Education and Care for Disadvantaged Children*, Bristol: Policy Press; see, for example, H. Penn and J. Sumison, in E. Lloyd and H. Penn (eds), *Childcare Markets* (2012), Bristol: Policy Press, pp. 19–42; 209–26.

5 H. Penn (2014), 'The Business of Childcare in Europe', *European Early Childhood Education Research Journal* 22(4): 432–56, 453.

6 Stewart et al., 'Common Challenges, Lessons for Policy', p. 223.

7 Gambaro et al., *An Equal Start?*, pp. 222–5.

8 OECD (2016), 'Society at a Glance 2016: OECD Social Indicators 2016', Paris: OECD.

9 Ibid.

10 Child Poverty Action Group (2013), 'New Investment in Childcare: Who Benefits?', *Poverty* 145: 6–8, 6.

11 K. Stewart (2013), 'Labour's Record on the Under 5s: Policy Spending and Outcomes 1997–2010',

Centre for Analysis of Social Exclusion, London: LSE.

12 J. de Henau (2017), 'Costing and Funding Free Universal Childcare of High Quality', WBG Childcare Briefing; J. M. Himmelweit et al. (2014), 'The Value of Childcare', London: NEF.

13 OECD (2011), 'Investing in High-Quality Childhood Education and Care (ECEC)', p. 4.

14 J. Aked et al. (2009), 'Backing the Future: Why Investing in Children is Good for Us All', London: NEF.

15 R. Wittenberg et al. (2018), 'Projections of Demand and Expenditure on Adult Social Care 2015 to 2040', *Personal Social Services Research Unit Discussion Paper* 2944(2): 6.

16 Conference Proceedings (2007), *Early Intervention and Older People: The Case for Preventative Services*, London: Kings College. https://www.kcl.ac.uk/scwru/mrc/makingresearchcountreport2610721.pdf.

17 Houses of Parliament (2018), 'Unpaid Care', POST PN 582, London: Houses of Parliament, p. 1.

18 D. Bouget et al. (2016), 'Work–Life Balance Measures for Persons of Working Age with Dependent Relatives in Europe: A Study of National Policies', Brussels: European Commission, p. 9.

19 R. Davies (2018), 'Profit Hungry Firms are Gambling on Social Care. Are the Stakes Too High?', *The Guardian*. https://www.theguardian.com/society/2018/feb/28/profit-hungry-firms-gambling-care-homes-stakes-too-high.

20 OECD (2018), 'Key Issues in Long-Term Care

Policy'. http://www.oecd.org/els/health-systems/long-term-care.htm.

21 Office for Budgetary Responsibility (2017), 'Fiscal Risks Report', London: Office for Budgetary Responsibility, p. 166.

22 R. Robertson et al. (2014), 'The Health and Social Care Systems of Nine Countries', Commission on the Future of Health and Social Care in England, London: King's Fund, p. 10.

23 D. Bell (2018), 'Free Personal Care: What the Scottish Approach to Social Care would Cost in England', The Health Foundation Newsletter.

24 Ibid.

25 S. Murphy (2018), 'Companies Running "Inadequate"' UK Care Homes Make £113m Profit', *The Guardian*. https://www.theguardian.com/society/2018/nov/23/revealed-companies-running-inadequate-uk-care-homes-make-113m-profit.

26 C. Glendinning and M. Wills (2018), 'What Can England Learn from the German Approach to Long-Term Care Funding?'. http://blogs.lse.ac.uk/politicsandpolicy/german-approach-to-long-term-care-funding/.

27 Department of Health and Social Care (2017), 'Adult Social Care: Quality Matters', London: DHSC.

Chapter 5 Rolling Out UBS:
Housing, Transport, Information

1 Ministry of Housing, Department for Communities and Local Government (2018), 'Dwelling Stock

Estimates: England, 2017', London: Ministry of Housing, Communities and Local Government.

2 The Marmot Review (2018), Strategic Review of Health Inequalities in England post-2010, London: Institute of Health Equity, p. 18.

3 N. Falk and J. Rudlin (2018), 'Learning from International Examples of Affordable Housing', London: Shelter, p. 9.

4 Ibid., p. 13.

5 D. Dorling, *All That Is Solid: How the Great Housing Disaster Defines our Times and What We Can Do about It*, London: Allen Lane, p. 114.

6 Social Prosperity Network (2017), 'Social Prosperity for the Future: A Proposal for Universal Basic Services', UCL: IGP, pp. 35–6, 42.

7 Falk and Rudlin, 'Learning from International Examples.'

8 OECD Affordable Housing Database (2019), 'Housing Costs over Income'.

9 A. Davis et al. (2018), 'A Minimum Income Standard for the UK 2008–2018: Continuity and Change', London: JRF; Rao and Min, 'Decent Living Standards'.

10 K. Bayliss and G. Mattioli (2018), 'Privatisation, Inequality and Poverty in the UK: Briefing Prepared for UN Rapporteur on Extreme Poverty and Human Rights', SRI Working Paper Series 116: 13–14.

11 Ibid., p. 14.

12 Ibid., p. 16.

13 R. Massey (2014), 'Boom in Free Bus Passes . . . but No Buses: Pensioner Perk so Popular Councils Forced

to Axe Services to Pay for It', *The Daily Mail*. https://www.dailymail.co.uk/news/article-2570718/Boom-free-bus-passes-no-buses-Pensioner-perk-popular-councils-forced-axe-services-pay-it.html.

14 Social Prosperity Network (2017), 'Social Prosperity for the Future', p. 26.

15 I. Taylor and L. Sloman (2016), 'Building a World Class Bus Service for Britain', London: Transport for Quality of Life, pp. 115–16.

16 Department for Transport (2016), 'Evaluation of Concessionary Bus Travel: The Impacts of the Free Bus Pass', London: Department for Transport.

17 KPMG (2017), 'The "True Value" of Local Bus Services: A Report to Greener Journeys', p. 12; R. Mackett (2015), 'Improving Accessibility for Older People – Investing in a Valuable Asset', *Journal of Transport & Health* 2(1): 5–13, 12; A. Jones et al. (2013), 'Entitlement to Concessionary Public Transport and Wellbeing: A Qualitative study of Young People and Older Citizens in London, UK', *Social Science & Medicine* 91: 202–9.

18 KPMG, 'The "True Value" of Local Bus Services', p. 17.

19 Greener Journeys (2016), 'The Value of the Bus to Society'. https://greenerjourneys.com/wp-content/uploads/2016/10/The-Value-of-the-Bus-to-Society-FINAL.pdf.

20 L. Sloman and L. Hopkinson (2019), 'Transforming Public Transport: Regulation, Spending and Free Buses for the Under 30s', London: Friends of the Earth, p. 6.

21 Department for Transport (2017), 'Transport Statistics Great Britain 2017: Energy and Environment', London: Department for Transport, p. 6.

22 K. Storchmann, (2003), 'Externalities by Automobiles and Fare-Free Transit in Germany – A Paradigm Shift?', *Journal of Public Transportation* 6(4): 89–105.

23 Rao and Min, 'Decent Living Standards', p. 225.

24 A. Davis et al. (2018), 'A Minimum Income Standard for the UK 2008–2018: Continuity and Change', London: JRF, p. 2.

25 UNHCR (2016), 'The Promotion, Protection and Enjoyment of Human Rights on the Internet', General Assembly A/HRC/32/L.20, p. 3.

26 Parliamentary Office of Science and Technology (2015), 'Trends in ICT', Post-Note 510: 2.

27 S. Dutta et al. (eds) (2015), 'The Global Information Technology Report 2015', World Economic Forum, p. xv.

28 OECD (2017), 'Internet Access'. https://data.oecd.org/ict/internet-access.htm.

29 K. Salemink, D. Strijker and G. Bosworth (2017), 'Rural Development in the Digital Age: A Systematic Literature Review on Unequal ICT Availability, Adoption, and Use in Rural Areas', *Journal of Rural Studies* 54: 360–71.

30 T. Hunt (2018), 'The Case for Universal Basic Infrastructure', in C. Berry (ed.), *What We Really Mean When We Talk about Industrial Strategy* (Future Economies), Manchester: Manchester Metropolitan University, p. 95.

31 R. D. Atkinson (2011), 'Economic Doctrines and Network Policy', *Telecommunications Policy* 35(5): 413–25.

32 Worldwide StatCounter, 'Desktop v Mobile Market Share Worldwide'. http://gs.statcounter. com/platform-market-share/desktop-mobile/world wide/#yearly-2010-2018.

33 European Commission (n.d.), 'Telecom Rules'. https://ec.europa.eu/digital-single-market/en/teleco ms-rules.

34 House of Commons Library (2018), 'A Universal Service Obligation for Broadband'. https://research briefings.parliament.uk/ResearchBriefing/Summary/ CBP-8146.

35 Sky UK (2019), 'Choose How Much Data You'd Like'. https://www.sky.com/shop/mobile/plans/data; Belong AU (2019), 'Explore Belong Sim Only Plans'. https:// www.belong.com.au/mobile/plans/small-sim-plan.

36 OECD (n.d.), 'Level of GDP Per Capita and Productivity'. https://stats.oecd.org/Index.aspx?Data SetCode=PDB_LV#.

37 See, for example, 'Apple Manufacturing in India for Indian Market to Accommodate Tariffs on Imports'. https://www.wsj.com/articles/apple-assembles-first-iphones-in-india-1495016276?mod=e2tw.

38 Lloyds Bank (2018), 'UK Consumer Digital Index 2018', pp. 16–27.

39 Connecting Devon and Somerset (n.d.). https://www. connectingdevonandsomerset.co.uk/#; Community Networks (n.d.), 'Community Network Map'. https://muninetworks.org/communitymap.

40 Guifi.net (n.d.), 'What is guifi.net?' http://guifi.net/
en/what_is_guifinet.

41 Magnolia Road (2018), Magnolia Road Internet
Cooperative. https://magnoliaroad.net.

42 T. Scholz (2016), 'Platform Cooperativism:
Challenging the Corporate Sharing Economy', Rosa
Luxemburg Stiftung, New York Office.

43 P. Koutroumpis (2018), 'The Economic Impact
of Broadband: Evidence from OECD Countries',
Ofcom, p. 14.

44 J. Perry et al. (2014), 'Emergency Use Only:
Understanding and Reducing the Use of Food Banks
in the UK', Oxford: Oxfam, pp. 7–13.

45 D. Taylor (2019), 'London Council Launches Free
School Meals Pilot Scheme', *The Guardian*. https://
www.theguardian.com/education/2019/jun/05/lond
on-council-launches-free-school-meals-pilot-scheme.

46 I. Lambert, 'Proud of Helsinki's Summer Playground
Meal Service for Kids'. Letters, *The Guardian*.
https://www.theguardian.com/world/2019/jun/04/pr
oud-of-helsinkis-summer-playground-meal-service-
for-kids.

Chapter 6 Challenges and Responses

1 See, for example, Froud and Williams, *Foundational
Economy*, pp. 123–30; S. Duffy (2018), 'Basic
Income or Basic Services', Centre for Welfare
Reform; B. Frankel (2018), *Fictions of Sustainability:
The Politics of Growth and Post Capitalist Futures*,
Melbourne: Greenmeadows, pp. 262–6.

2 B. Born and M. Purcell (2006), 'Avoiding the Local Trap: Scale and Food Systems in Planning Research', *Journal of Planning Education and Research* 26(2): 195–207.

3 Evergreen Cooperatives (n.d.), 'About Us'. https://www.evgoh.com/about-us/.

4 A. Coote (2017), 'Building a New Social Commons', London: NEF, pp. 14–15.

5 The Citizens' Assembly (n.d.), 'Welcome to the Citizens' Assembly'. https://www.citizensassembly.ie/en/.

6 M. Mersch (ed.) (2018), 'Wellbeing for Everyone in a Sustainable Europe'. Independent Commission on Sustainable Equality, p. 75.

7 Froud and Williams, *Foundational Economy*, p. 111.

8 J. Kellas (1992), 'The Scottish Constitutional Convention', in *The Scottish Government Yearbook*, Edinburgh: University of Edinburgh.

9 This figure splits the difference between the cost of free bus passes for all and extending Transport for London's service across the United Kingdom.

10 OECD (2019), General government spending (indicator), doi: 10.1787/a31cbf4d-en.

11 Ibid.

12 OECD comparative revenue statistics. https://stats.oecd.org/viewhtml.aspx?datasetcode=REV&lang=en.

13 I. Gough (2017), *Heat, Greed and Human Need*, Cheltenham: Edward Elgar, p. 162; D. Fell (2016), *Bad Habits, Hard Choices: Using the Tax System to Make Us Healthier*, London: London Publishing Partnership, pp. 106–10.

Conclusions

1 J. Stiglitz (2017), 'Austerity has Strangled Britain. Only Labour Will Consign It to History', *The Guardian*. https://www.theguardian.com/commentis free/2017/jun/07/austerity-britain-labour-neoliberal ism-reagan-thatcher.

2 D. Phillips et al. (2018), 'British Social Attitudes: The 35th Report', London: The National Centre for Social Research.

3 OECD (2018), 'Risks that Matter', OECD. http://www.oecd.org/els/soc/Risks-That-Matter-2018-Ma in Findings.pdf.

4 B. Meuleman et al. (2018), 'The Past, Present and Future of European Welfare Attitudes: Topline Results from Round 8 of the European Social Survey', *European Social Survey Topline Results Series* 8: 4.

5 A. Simms and P. Newell (2019), *How Did We Do That? The Possibility of Radical Transition*, Brighton: Radical Transition Alliance, p. 5.

6 Froud and Williams, *Foundational Economy*, p. 130.

7 Congressional Western Congress (2019), 'Green New Deal', 116th Congress 1st Session, H. Res. 109.

Index

Index

Index

Index

Index

Index

Index

Index

Index